Lake Erie

Conneaut

HEADLAND DUNES
STATE NATURE
RESERVE

Pair

Mentor
Eastlake
Lake
Euclid
Willoughby

East
Rese

Geauga

PUN
SP

Lakewood
Cleveland
Euclid

Lorain
North
Olmsted
Cuyahoga
Garfield
Heights
Solon
Akron
City Res.

GRAND
RIVER WA

Mosquito
Creek L.
Cortland

Elyria
Parma
Strongsville
Twinsburg

Trumbull

Shenango
River Lake

Oberlin
Hudson
Portage
Warren

Lorain
Brunswick
Michael J.
Kirwan
Reservoir
Meander
Cr. Res.
Hubbard

CUYAHOGA
VALLEY NP
Stow

FINDLEY
SP
Medina
Medina
Cuyahoga
Falls

WEST
BRANCH SP

LAKE
MILTON
SP
Youngstown

Akron
Campbell

Ashland
Barberton
Summit
Mogadore
Reservoir
Canfield

Portage
Lakes

BERLIN
LAKE WA
Berlin
Lake
Mahoning

Ashland
Wayne
Alliance
Salem

Wooster
Massillon
Canton

Stark

Columbiana

BEAVER
CREEK SP

field
and

Mohicanville
Reservoir

KILLBUCK
MARSH
WILDLIFE
AREA

HIGHLANDTOWN
WA

East
Liverpool

MORICAN
EMORIAL
SF

Holmes

nox
on

Dover
Atwood
Lake
Carroll

BRUSH
CREEK WA

New
Philadelphia
Leesville
Lake

JEFFERSON
LAKE SP

Mohawk
Reservoir
Coshocton
Tuscarawas

Harrison
Jefferson
Steubenville

king

WOODBURY
WA
Coshocton

Clendining
Lake

FERNWOOD
SF

ewark
ath

Wills
Creek
Lake

SALT
FORK SP
Piedmont
Lake

EGYPT
VALLEY WA
Martins
Ferry

DILLON
SP
Salt
Fork
Lake

keye
ke

Dillon
Lake
TRI-VALLEY
WA

Zanesville
Cambridge

BARKCAMP
SP

Muskingum
Guernsey
Belmont

PERRY
SP

Senecaville
Lake

WOLF RUN
SP

MONROE
LAKE WA

Perry

JESSE
OWENS
WA
Noble
Monroe

CONSOL ENERGY
POWHATAN
POINT WA

Logan
Morgan

WAYNE
NF

Muskingum

BURR OAK
SP
Burr Oak
Reservoir

WAYNE
NF

king

STROUDS
RUN SP
Washington
Marietta

ZALESKI
SF
WAYNE
NF

ton
Athens
Belpre

Athens

FORKED
RUN SP

Meigs

Gallia

ROWN
TY WA

nce

PENNSYLVANIA

WEST
VIRGINIA

Ohio R.

American Birding Association

Field Guide

to Birds of

Ohio

Ethan Kistler

PHOTOGRAPHS BY
Brian E. Small
AND OTHERS

Scott & Nix, Inc.
NEW YORK

PUBLISHED BY SCOTT & NIX, INC.
150 W 28TH ST, STE 1900
NEW YORK, NY 10001
SCOTTANDNIX.COM

FIRST EDITION 2019
SECOND PRINTING 2024

ISBN 978-1-935622-70-3

AMERICAN BIRDING ASSOCIATION, INC.
800-850-2473
ABA.ORG

SCOTT & NIX, INC. BOOKS
ARE DISTRIBUTED TO THE TRADE BY

INDEPENDENT PUBLISHERS GROUP (IPG)
814 NORTH FRANKLIN STREET
CHICAGO, IL 60610
800-888-4741
IPGBOOK.COM

Contents

The American Birding Association inspires all people to enjoy and protect wild birds.

The ABA represents the North American birding community and supports birders through publications, conferences, workshops, events, partnerships, and networks.

The ABA's education programs promote birding skills, ornithological knowledge, and the development of and implementation of a conservation ethic.

The ABA encourages birders to apply their skills to help conserve birds and their habitats, and we represent the interests of birders in planning and legislative arenas.

We welcome all birders as members.

THE AMERICAN BIRDING ASSOCIATION
CODE OF ETHICS

Everyone who enjoys birds and birding must always respect wildlife, its environment, and the rights of others. In any conflict of interest between birds and birders, the welfare of the birds and their environment comes first.

CODE OF BIRDING ETHICS

1. Promote the welfare of birds and their environment.

1(a) Support the protection of important bird habitat.

1(B) To avoid stressing birds or exposing them to danger, exercise restraint and caution during observation, photography, sound recording, or filming.

Limit the use of recordings and other methods of attracting birds, and never use such methods in heavily birded areas, or for attracting any species that is Threatened, Endangered,

or of Special Concern, or is rare in your local area; Keep
well back from nests and nesting colonies, roosts, display areas,
and important feeding sites. In such sensitive areas, if there
is a need for extended observation, photography, filming,
or recording, try to use a blind or hide, and take advantage of
natural cover.

Use artificial light sparingly for filming or photography,
especially for close-ups.

1(c)Before advertising the presence of a rare bird, evaluate
the potential for disturbance to the bird, its surroundings,
and other people in the area, and proceed only if access
can be controlled, disturbance minimized, and permission
has been obtained from private land-owners. The sites
of rare nesting birds should be divulged only to the proper
conservation authorities.

1(d)Stay on roads, trails, and paths where they exist;
otherwise keep habitat disturbance to a minimum.

2. Respect the law, and the rights of others.

2(a)Do not enter private property without the owner's
explicit permission.

2[B]Follow all laws, rules, and regulations governing use of
roads and public areas, both at home and abroad.

2(c)Practice common courtesy in contacts with other people.
Your exemplary behavior will generate goodwill with birders
and non-birders alike.

3. Ensure that feeders, nest structures, and other artificial bird
environments are safe.

3(a)Keep dispensers, water, and food clean, and free of decay
or disease. It is important to feed birds continually during
harsh weather.

3[B]Maintain and clean nest structures regularly.

3(c)If you are attracting birds to an area, ensure the birds
are not exposed to predation from cats and other domestic
animals, or dangers posed by artificial hazards.

4. Group birding, whether organized or impromptu, requires
special care.

Each individual in the group, in addition to the obligations spelled out in Items 1 and 2, has responsibilities as a Group Member.

4(a)Respect the interests, rights, and skills of fellow birders, as well as people participating in other legitimate outdoor activities. Freely share your knowledge and experience, except where code 1(c) applies. Be especially helpful to beginning birders.

4[B]If you witness unethical birding behavior, assess the situation, and intervene if you think it prudent. When interceding, inform the person(s) of the inappropriate action, and attempt, within reason, to have it stopped. If the behavior continues, document it, and notify appropriate individuals or organizations.

Group Leader Responsibilities [amateur and professional trips and tours].

4(c)Be an exemplary ethical role model for the group. Teach through word and example.

4(d)Keep groups to a size that limits impact on the environment, and does not interfere with others using the same area.

4(e)Ensure everyone in the group knows of and practices this code.

4(f)Learn and inform the group of any special circumstances applicable to the areas being visited (e.g. no tape recorders allowed).

4(g)Acknowledge that professional tour companies bear a special responsibility to place the welfare of birds and the benefits of public knowledge ahead of the company's commercial interests. Ideally, leaders should keep track of tour sightings, document unusual occurrences, and submit records to appropriate organizations.

Everyone who enjoys birds and birding must always respect wildlife, its environment, and the rights of others. The ABA Code of Ethics should be read, followed, and shared by all birders.

Please follow this code and distribute and teach it to others.

The American Birding Association's Code of Birding Ethics may be freely reproduced for distribution/dissemination. An electronic version may be found at aba.org/about/ethics.

Foreword

Ohio is a great state for birding with a wealth of prime habitats for birds and outstanding opportunities for birders of all levels. Like all the guides in this series, this book can help you do whatever you want with birding. Perhaps you enjoy birds a few days a year in your yard or local park and just want to know a little more about them and to know some of their names. Or maybe you want to dive deeper and really get familiar with the hundreds of amazing birds that call Ohio home for part or all of each year. Our aim is to meet you where you are and give you useful, reliable information and insight into birds and birding.

Author Ethan Kistler is the perfect guide for those wanting to explore the birds of Ohio. You're in very good hands with him. The gorgeous photography by Brian Small and others will not only to aid your identifications—it will inspire you to get out and see more of these beautiful and fascinating creatures for yourself.

I invite you to visit the American Birding Association website (aba.org), where you'll find a wealth of free resources and ways to connect with the birding community that will also help you get the most from your birding in Ohio and beyond. Please consider becoming an ABA member yourself—one of the best parts of birding is joining a community of fun, passionate people.

Now get on out there! Enjoy this book. Enjoy Ohio. And most of all, enjoy birding!

Good birding,

Jeffrey A. Gordon

Jeffrey A. Gordon, *President*
American Birding Association

Birds in Ohio

When birders plan a birding holiday within the United States, states such as Florida, Texas, Arizona, California, and Colorado typically come to mind and for good reason. However, Ohio offers fantastic birding opportunities and is one of the most underrated birding destinations in the country.

Because of its location between Lake Erie and the Ohio River Valley, many bird species converge in Ohio where the west meets the east and the north meets the south. In the state's northeastern counties, scattered hemlock gorges host breeding boreal species such as Canada Warbler, Winter Wren, and Dark-eyed Junco. The unglaciated foothills of the Appalachian Mountains in southeastern Ohio offer extensive deciduous forests where Kentucky and Worm-eating Warblers, Mississippi Kites, and Summer Tanagers reach their northern limits.

Ohio's official state bird is the colorful Northern Cardinal.

In western Ohio, birders can find Lark Sparrows, Bell's Vireos, Black-necked Stilts, and Dickcissels at the eastern edge of their range.

The real magic, however, is Ohio's geographic position where many species traveling from both northeastern and north-western breeding grounds converge, offering spectacular concentrations of migrants. The renowned Magee Marsh boardwalk on the edge of Lake Erie is one of the most famous migration hotspots on the continent. It comes as no surprise that the largest birding festival in the Western Hemisphere,

Dark-eyed Juncos are common statewide in winter, but restricted to northeast Ohio during summer.

"The Biggest Week in American Birding," is hosted here every May. This region attracts more than 50,000 people who travel from every state and many other countries to experience migration at its finest. It is possible to see 25 species of warblers in a single day, watch flocks of shorebirds feeding on mudflats, and look skyward to witness kettles of Broad-winged Hawks and other raptors overhead.

Ohio birders have always known the excitement of birding in the state, and now birders from elsewhere are flocking to the state to enjoy the spectacle.

The Magnolia Warbler is just one of a over 30 warblers possible to see at Magee Marsh.

Birds in this Guide

The official list of birds in Ohio is approaching 440 species. A third of these are very rare and some have been seen only once or twice. This guide includes the nearly 280 species found annually in the state plus a few rarities that are regularly observed.

The species sequence in this field guide loosely follows the current taxonomic order (as of July 2019), with a few birds out of sequence. The guide's purpose is to aid beginning and intermediate birders. When two species are very similar, they are typically placed next to each other for comparison.

Although more commonly found throughout the Western U.S., Gulf Coast, and Atlantic Coast, Black-necked Stilts have recently expanded their range into Ohio.

Identifying Birds

When identifying a bird, our first instinct is to look at its color. Although this may work for some species, it is not always the key to identification. Not all Northern Cardinals are red, not all Bald Eagles have a white head, and Black-bellied Plovers don't always have a black belly. Before consulting a field guide, it is best to observe the bird for as long as possible. New birders will often look at a bird briefly and then quickly start thumbing through their guide. They may soon realize that there are similar species, but if the bird has flown away, key features for identification are gone. Watch the bird's features carefully before turning to the field guide.

Black-bellied Plovers don't always have a black belly.

Your first step is to note the GISS (General Impressions, Size, and Shape) of the bird. This phrase is commonly used by birders. What was your general impression– Was it a sparrow– A duck– Perhaps a shorebird– Then, move on to size. Typically, we compare size to a bird we are familiar with. Is it the size of a sparrow– A crow– Or large like an eagle– How about the shape– Is it tall, slender, or short and plump– Did it have a deeply forked tail like a Barn Swallow's or a stubby tail like a swift's– In flight, were the wings broad or bent at the "wrist"– Noting these general features will point you in the right direction.

Next, consider habitat. While many birds may look similar, they often occur in specific habitats. For an example, Swamp Sparrows are almost always in a damp or marshy area. Grass-

Swamp Sparrows are specific to wet, marshy habitats.

hopper Sparrows, in contrast, occur in open grasslands. Woodpeckers are most often near woodlands, while Horned Larks prefer open country. In this field guide, I include habitats for each species to emphasize a bird's specific ecological "niche."

Don't forget to focus on "the small things." Nearly all birds can be narrowed down simply by looking at their bills. Each species specializes in a certain food or feeding behavior. For example, shorebirds have long bills for probing into mud for crustaceans. Hummingbirds use their uniquely long bills to sip nectar from flowers. Seed eaters such as grosbeaks and cardinals have very strong thick bills that can crush seeds open. Other birds such as warblers have small thin bills for gleaning insects from leaves. Hawks, eagles, and even the Northern Shrike have specialized sharp, hooked bills for tearing flesh of birds, mammals, insects, and fish. Paying attention to the bill size and shape is one key to narrowing down your identification.

The specialized hooked bill of the Northern Shrike is an excellent clue to the identification of this predatory songbird

The Parts of a Bird

Learning basic bird anatomy is essential to identification. Using this field guide, you will note various terms used to describe parts of a bird. Most of these are self-explanatory such as head, bill, and wings, but others are not so straightforward. Before using this guide, I recommend looking over the diagrams and terms on the following few pages.

PARTS OF A DUCK
Male Blue-winged Teal.

wing tip

back

nape

crown

forehead

bill

breast

tail

flank

side

neck

undertail

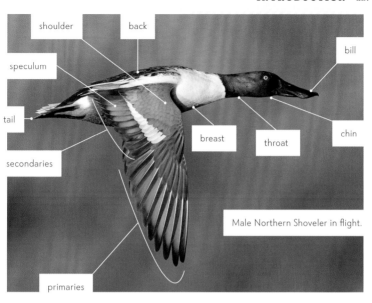

shoulder

back

bill

speculum

tail

secondaries

breast

throat

chin

Male Northern Shoveler in flight.

primaries

crown

forehead

nape

PARTS OF A GULL
Adult Ring-billed Gull.

throat

back

neck

breast

belly

foot

wing tip

tail

toes

PARTS OF A RAPTOR
Red-tailed Hawk in flight.

underwing coverts

leading edge

primaries

bend of wing

secondaries

thigh

belly band

trailing edge

PARTS OF A BIRD OF PREY
Adult male American Kestrel.

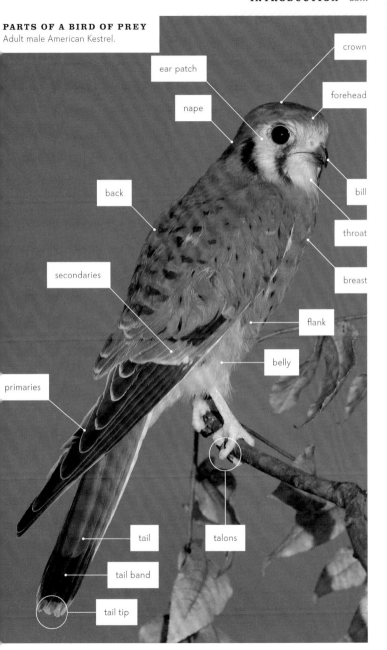

crown

ear patch

forehead

nape

bill

throat

back

breast

secondaries

flank

belly

primaries

tail

talons

tail band

tail tip

PARTS OF A SONGBIRD
Blue-headed Vireo

eye ring

crown

lores

nape

chin

back

throat

breast

secondaries

wing bar

primaries

flanks

tail

uppertail coverts

undertail coverts

belly

Yellow-rumped Warbler

cheek patch

eyebrow/supercillium

nape

forehead

greater primary coverts

eye crescent/eye arc

shoulder

rump

flanks

undertail coverts

primary projection

A Year of Birding in Ohio

Ohio's geographic location situated in the Midwest and Great Lakes regions offers four distinct seasons. The birdlife changes just as quickly as the seasons. Below is a summary of what to expect each month, recommendations on where to go birding, and what to look for.

JANUARY is the dead of winter and our coldest and snowiest month. In northeastern Ohio, the "snow belt" can be relentlessly frigid. While most people stay indoors, birding can be rewarding. Your best bet is to head to any open body of water where large concentrations of waterfowl may be found. For gull enthusiasts, the Lake Erie lakefront, particularly in the Cleveland region, hosts large concentrations of gulls, which can yield rare or unusual species. Snowy Owls may be found in the northern part of the state along Lake Erie or in rural open farmlands. The Cleveland Burke Lakefront Airport is probably the most reliable place in the state to see this arctic owl.

Snowy Owl ranks high on peoples list of birds to see in winter.

Driving quiet farm roads can turn up mixed flocks of Horned Larks, Snow Buntings, and Lapland Longspurs in open fields, especially if manure was recently laid. For the more fair-weather birders, this is an excellent season to sit back and watch your bird feeders from the comfort of home. After recent snowfalls, bird numbers spike at feeders and during "irruption" years when food shortages up north send winter finches south.

FEBRUARY is similar to January with short days, cold temperatures, and frequent snowstorms. Gull concentrations continue along the Lake Erie shoreline while waterfowl numbers begin to increase during the second half of the month. Some of our earliest migrants start arriving near the end of February including Killdeer, American Woodcock, Common Grackles, Red-winged Blackbirds, and early Tree Swallows and Eastern Phoebes.

Some winters, northern finches invade south such as this Red Crossbill.

MARCH is when waterfowl migration peaks statewide as lakes and wetlands thaw. The Lake Erie region can have impressive flights of ducks, geese, and swans. Raptor migration becomes evident, with flights of Red-shouldered Hawks, Turkey Vultures, and Bald Eagles moving north on days with warm southerly winds. The second half of March is when we start to see arrivals of shorebirds including Dunlin, Pectoral Sandpiper, and both yellowlegs. On the passerine front, Eastern Phoebes are joined by Fox Sparrows, Golden-crowned Kinglets, and the first Louisiana Waterthrushes and Pine Warblers. American Woodcocks are also in full "skydance" mode.

APRIL brings a noticeable increase in numbers and diversity. Waterfowl numbers continue but will gradually decline through the month. Wetlands come alive with Red-winged Blackbirds on territory, Virginia Rails skulking in the vegeta-

Marshes come alive in early spring with male Red-winged Blackbirds defending their territories.

tion, and Green Herons fishing from the shoreline. Shorebird and raptor movements continue to increase, the first Chimney Swifts arrive and are followed quickly by Ruby-throated Hummingbirds. By the last week of April, the first of most species begin arriving, especially migrants from the tropics such as vireos, warblers, and flycatchers.

MAY makes Ohio famous. People worldwide travel to northwestern Ohio to one of the best migration hotspots in North America, though the migration is not limited to this region. Woodlots burst with the songs and colors of warblers, tanagers, orioles, grosbeaks, and buntings. Some of the earlier migrants will be gone by the end of the first week including Winter Wren, Hermit Thrush, and Rusty Blackbird. Come mid-May, diversity peaks and soon later arrivals appear such as the elusive Connecticut Warbler and many flycatchers including Olive-sided and Yellow-bellied. By the end of the month, the trees leaf out making it more difficult to spot birds, and migration begins to decline. Shorebirds, on the other hand, are still migrating through in excellent numbers.

Olive-sided Flycatchers typically migrate much later in spring than other birds.

JUNE bids farewell to lingering migrants by the end of the first week. Shorebird migration continues through the first half of the month while virtually all migrating waterfowl have departed. June is the peak of the breeding season when resident passerines are in full song and display. Although most northern migrants are gone, this is still an excellent time to go birding — a time to appreciate special local breeders such as Cerulean, Hooded, and Kentucky Warblers, Scarlet Tanagers, and Bobolinks.

JULY sees a quick reduction in song activity as this is the hottest month after most species have had their first broods and are actively feeding their young. Southbound shorebird migrants increase in numbers during mid- to late July. Some of Ohio's breeding residents begin to head south, including Louisiana Waterthrush and Kentucky Warbler.

During the summer, birds such as this Hooded Warbler, are actively feeding young

AUGUST is hot and humid but an excellent time to look for rare shorebirds. Try scanning any open mudflats or beaches such as Conneaut, Howard Marsh Metropark, and Hoover Reservoir. Some of our flycatchers, namely Acadian and Least, have already begun heading south, disappearing before anyone notices. These are joined by Orchard Orioles, Grasshopper Sparrows, and other early departures. The last week of August brings the first southbound warblers, which are drabber and more silent than they were in the spring.

SEPTEMBER offers more excellent shorebirding statewide. Some species such as Baird's Sandpiper, Hudsonian Godwit, and Buff-breasted Sandpiper are virtually absent in spring and are more likely to be found in fall. Neotropical migrants such as warblers, vireos, and thrushes peak in numbers while flycatchers and swallow numbers decline through the month. Early winter arrivals start to show up including Red-breasted Nuthatch, Brown Creeper, Winter Wren, Golden-crowned Kinglet, and White-throated Sparrow. September is also a great month for finding rarities. A boat trip on Lake Erie may even turn up a Long-tailed Jaeger or Sabine's Gull if you're lucky.

September is an excellent month for shorebirding. Baird's Sandpiper like this one are more regular than in spring.

OCTOBER is a pleasant time of year for birding in Ohio with mild temperatures and peak fall colors. Nearly all flycatchers are gone by now, but shorebirds, vireos, warblers, and thrushes are still moving through and most will depart by the end of the month. In this month of transition, they are replaced by increasing numbers of waterfowl, Common Loons, Bonaparte's Gulls, and American Tree Sparrows. For those looking for a challenge, October offers your best chance at finding the infrequent Nelson's and LeConte's Sparrows in the state. Search for them in damp meadows and shallow grassy marshes where they skulk.

With dedication, birders may find a Nelson's Sparrow, a scarce migrant in Ohio during the month of October in damp meadows and shallow marshes.

NOVEMBER can be harsh with wind and cold temperatures. Most fall migration has ended, although a few warblers and shorebirds linger into the first week. Any hummingbirds seen this late in the year are likely a vagrant species from the west because Ruby-throated Hummingbirds are typically gone by now, but it's worth keeping your nectar feeders up. Waterfowl numbers peak, and impressive numbers of Tundra Swans can be found, especially in northwestern Ohio where numbers stage in the thousands. Sea ducks and diving ducks become more prevalent on Lake Erie and large inland lakes. Uncommon winter residents such as Rough-legged Hawk, Northern Shrike, Snowy and Short-eared Owls, and winter finches can be found. With patience, rare gulls may be located among large concentrations of other gulls along Lake Erie and nearby landfills. By the end of the month, November feels like the dead of winter.

By November uncommon sea ducks such as this Black Scoter, can be found along the Lake Erie lakefront.

DECEMBER is the cloudiest month as winter sets in and when we typically see our first substantial snowfall. Nearly all migrants have departed except waterfowl. Large concentrations of ducks, geese, and swans can remain in the state through the month, but during colder winters when lakes freeze over, they may push farther south. The second half of December is dominated by Christmas Bird Counts, the nation's longest running citizen-science bird census. Contact your local organizer and participate. Many of these counts turn up rare and unusual species as countless birders scour urban and wild environments.

The second half of December is when birders participate in Christmas Bird Counts where populations trends of species can be recorded, such as the Red-breasted Nuthatch.

Resources for Ohio Birders

ONLINE RESOURCES

eBird (ebird.org)
The largest biodiversity-related citizen-science database in the world, eBird is the ultimate resource for birders. Birders can upload their personal bird lists, photos, and audio recordings, see real-time information on recent sightings, and look at past records to gain knowledge of bird distribution, seasonality, and abundance. This invaluable resource can be used locally in Ohio and worldwide. Keep track of your sightings and plan your future birding trips –and it's free.

Ohio-birds Listserv
birding.aba.org/maillist/OH
A public email list you can subscribe to and share and learn of other sightings in Ohio, receive rare bird alerts, ask questions about birding in Ohio, and discuss the ecology of Ohio birds.

Facebook
A variety of Facebook groups are available to join, which are related to birds and birding in Ohio.

facebook.com/groups/BirdingOhio allows birders to share current sightings, pictures, and videos; to share thoughts and ideas about birding; to ask questions about bird identification, status and distribution, and birding locations.

facebook.com/groups/1504363176528360/ Ohio Chase Birds is a non-discussion group used solely for sharing and updating others on rare bird sightings.

facebook.com/groups/CentralOhioBirders/ This is a regional discussion page for Central Ohio birders.

CLUBS

American Birding Association (aba.org)
The ABA is a non-profit organization that provides leadership to birders by increasing knowledge, skills, and enjoyment of birding. This is the most important organization in North America that specifically caters to recreational birders. The ABA also contributes to bird and bird habitat conservation.

Ohio Ornithological Society (ohiobirds.org)
Welcoming backyard birders and researchers alike into the field, the Ohio Ornithological Society is the only statewide organization specifically devoted to fostering a deeper appreciation of wild birds, fellowship, and collaboration in advancing our collective knowledge and our ability to speak with one voice to preserve Ohio's bird habitats.

Black Swamp Bird Observatory (bsbo.org)
The mission of the Black Swamp Bird Observatory is to inspire the appreciation, enjoyment, and conservation of birds and their habitats through research, education, and outreach. The BSBO organizes the annual "Biggest Week in American Birding" festival in northwestern Ohio and oversees the Ohio Young Birders Club.

Ohio Young Birders Club (ohioyoungbirders.org)
The Ohio Young Birders Club was developed by the Black Swamp Bird Observatory in 2006 to encourage, educate, and empower our youth conservation leaders. Each month student members can participate in field trips to exciting places in Ohio. In addition to field trips and outings, members participate in service projects focused on habitat restoration and conservation. For ages 12-18, the OYBC holds an annual young birders conference and has regional chapters.

The Audubon Society (audubon.org)
The National Audubon Society protects birds and the places they need, today and tomorrow, throughout the Americas using science, advocacy, education, and on-the-ground conservation. Audubon's state programs, nature centers, chapters, and partners have an unparalleled wingspan that reaches millions of people to inform, inspire, and unite diverse communities in conservation action.

PRINTED MATERIALS

The Sibley Guide to Birds, 2nd Edition (2014)
Kaufman Field Guide to Birds of North America (2005)
The Second Atlas of Breeding Birds in Ohio (2016)
National Geographic Field Guide to the Birds of North America, 7th Edition (2017)

American Birding Association

Field Guide to
Birds of Ohio

Snow Goose

Chen caerulescens

L 27-33" | **WS** 54"

The Snow Goose nests in the high Arctic during the summer months and is an uncommon migrant across Ohio. Most sightings occur in the state between October and March with some birds lingering well into May. While in Ohio, they may be found in marshes, rivers, reservoirs, and farm fields. Hundreds and occasionally thousands may be seen along the western boundary of the state on the edge of the Mississippi flyway during the spring and fall. They have a distinctive flight pattern of irregular wavy lines, unlike the V-formation of other geese. Elsewhere in the state, singletons to a few dozen individuals can sporadically be seen mixed with larger Canada Geese, with smaller numbers remaining throughout the winter. This species has two color morphs, "blue" and "white," and Ohio tends to see a nice mix of both.

Bill shows obvious "grin patch" seen well in both color morphs.

All-white, medium-sized goose with black wing tips.

"Blue morph" sooty gray overall with a contrasting white head and gray wings.

Ross's Goose

Chen rossii

L 23" | **WS** 45"

A smaller version of the Snow Goose, the diminutive Ross's Goose is not much larger than a Mallard. Ross's occurs in the state from October to early May, and your best chance of finding this scarce species is by searching through flocks of Snow Geese for a smaller individual or by finding one that is dwarfed by Canada Geese. Unlike the Snow Goose, the "blue morph" of the Ross's Goose is very rare and unlikely to be seen. When not accompanied by Snow Geese for size comparison, it is quickly told apart by its lack of "grin patch" on its bill.

All-white small goose with black wing tips and without a "grin patch."

Greater White-fronted Goose

Anser albifrons

L 25-32" **WS** 66"

This medium-sized, brownish-gray goose is an uncommon migrant and winter resident across much of the state, favoring open farm fields, lakes, and wetlands. They may be found from October through March, with smaller numbers lingering into May. Listen for their two-to three-syllable high-pitched honk with a laughing quality. Caution is needed not to confuse this species with the similar domestic Graylag Goose. Graylag lacks the black belly blotches of Greater White-fronted, shows no white on the face, and has a more "pot-bellied" look.

Gray goose with white on face, orange bill and legs, and black blotches on the belly.

Canada Goose

Branta canadensis

L 30-43" | **WS** 50-67"

The ubiquitous Canada Goose is common in every part of the
state from bodies of water to farm fields, golf courses, and
well-manicured lawns. Ohio has two distinctive populations.
The resident "Giant" subspecies was introduced and became
an established resident across the state. They tend to be more
accustomed to the presence of humans and they frequently nest
in city parks and golf courses. This goose aggressively protects
nesting sites and will chase away intruders with loud "hissing."
The migratory population, which breeds in northern Canada,
passes through Ohio from February to March and again from
October to December, when large flocks in V-formation can fill
the sky with their familiar *h-runk* calls.

Large, black neck and head,
and obvious white chin strap.

Cackling Goose

Branta hutchsinii

L 25" | **WS** 51"

Once conidered the same species as the Canada Goose, the
Cackling Goose was split into its own species in 2004. It is the
smaller of the two and is an uncommon migrant and winter
resident. They turn up just about anywhere in Ohio, becoming
scarcer to the southeast. Persistent birders may sometimes be
rewarded by sifting through flocks of hundreds or thousands
of Canada Geese to find one or more Cackling. Their calls are
a more musical, toned-down version of the emphatic Canada
Goose. Confusion with Canada Goose is common. Note that
Cackling is generally much smaller, closer to the size of a
Mallard, and has a stubbier bill.

Smaller goose with stubby
bill, thick short neck, and
obviously steeper forehead.

Brant

Branta bernicla

L 23" | **WS** 45"

Brant are primarily found along the coastlines of the Atlantic and Pacific Oceans. However, a small number pass through the Great Lakes each fall on their way to the East Coast from their tundra breeding grounds. In Ohio, the majority are observed from late October through mid-November from Cleveland east along the Lake Erie coastline. Very few are seen outside this brief window of time, and rarely do they stray inland to large bodies of water. This small gray goose with a black head, neck, breast, and obvious white in the tail sets this species apart.

Small goose with gray belly, black head, neck, and breast, white necklace, and white tail.

Mute Swan

Cygnus olor

L 50–60" | **WS** 82–94"

Native to Europe and Asia, the elegant Mute Swan was brought
to North America in the 1800s as a decorative waterfowl for
ponds and lakes. Unfortunately, this species is now considered highly invasive. It will out-compete our native waterfowl
for nesting sites and their intensive feeding habits have had a
detrimental effect on food availability for native birds, water
quality, and erosion control. First recorded in Ohio near Akron
in 1911, they did not start breeding in the state until the late
1980s at Ottawa NWR. Since then, their numbers have exploded
and may be seen throughout the state. Contrary to its name,
they do make a variety of calls including hisses and snorts,
especially when provoked. In flight, the Mute Swan produces
a rhythmic whistling sound with the wings, unlike our other
swans.

Large white swan with an orange
bill, unique among our swans

Trumpeter Swan

Cygnus buccinator

L 54-62" | **WS** 80"

Once extirpated from Ohio, reintroductions began in 1996 when the first birds were released at Magee Marsh Wildlife Area. This was followed by ten other sites across the northern part of the state over the next ten years. This reintroduction program ended in success with Trumpeter Swans now being found across Ohio, though they remain absent from the southeast. Unlike Mute Swans, the Trumpeter Swan prefers nesting away from humans normally in lakes and large wetland areas. The largest and one of the heaviest waterfowl species in the state, they can be found year-round in Ohio. As their name suggests, their call is reminiscent of someone just learning to play a trumpet.

Large white swan with long straight black bill. The feathers on the forehead come to a point above the bill.

Tundra Swan

Cygnus columbianus

L 52" | **WS** 66"

A swan from the high arctic, we begin to see this migrant passing over Ohio around late October when flocks can reach the hundreds or even thousands as they head toward the East Coast. Flocks are often detected by their distinctive *kloo* barking call as they fly over in V-formation. A large number remain in Ohio throughout the winter, spending their time in open farmlands, marshes and reservoirs. They normally depart Ohio by early April. Try searching at Killdeer Plains and Killbuck Marsh Wildlife Areas and the NW Ohio marshes (Ottawa NWR and Magee Marsh). The smallest of our three swans, they are best distinguished by the yellow spot at the base of their black bill. Any black-billed swan in Ohio during the summer would be the similar Trumpeter Swan.

Our smallest swan with a yellow spot at the base of their black bill. Unlike the Trumpeter Swan, the edge of the feathers on the forehead are rounded above the bill.

Young birds quite dusky overall.

Wood Duck

Aix sponsa

L 20" | **WS** 27"

Arguably our most attractive waterfowl, the Wood Duck is a common migrant and summer breeder, although a small number remain throughout the winter. Preferring flooded woodland, marshes, ponds, and slow-moving rivers, Wood Ducks nest in old woodpecker holes and man-made duck boxes. After hatching, the ducklings take a leap of faith and jump out of their nesting cavity onto the ground or water below, sometimes from as high as 40 feet. Unlikely to be confused with any other duck, the males showcase a stunning array of iridescent greens and chestnut with an obvious crest. Females are far less colorful. When disturbed, females give alarming *oo-eek oo-eek* calls, while the male produces a rising and falling *jaweep*.

Male unmistakable with green crest and back, chestnut breast, white markings, and red bill and eyes.

Less colorful than the male but the white oval marking around the eye is distinctive.

Blue-winged Teal

Anas discors

L 15" | **WS** 23"

A small dabbling duck, Blue-winged Teal favor marshes and small lakes where they feed on submerged vegetation and aquatic insects. In Ohio we see the greatest numbers during spring (March-April) and fall (August-October) migration. A good number remain during the summer where they nest in wetlands across the state. Known as long-distance migrants, a large number overwinter along the Gulf Coast, but some travel as far as South America. However, a handful do over-winter in Ohio, probably departing once no open bodies of water remain. Males give a high *peew* call, while the females give a typical quack.

Males have an obvious white crescent on their dark head and white hip patches.

Female is very plain mottled brown overall. Note the darkish cap and eyeline.

Northern Shoveler

Anas clypeata

L 19" | **WS** 31"

With its spatulate-shaped bill, green head, and rufous flanks, the male Northern Shoveler is not easily confused with any other duck. They are commonly seen in Ohio during migration when the vast majority move through between late February and early May in the spring and August to December in the fall. During the winter, concentrations of about a dozen individuals can be seen on open bodies of water until the waters freeze over. In the summer, shovelers are uncommon in the state. You can occasionally find a single individual or a breeding pair, mainly in the western Lake Erie basin. Their preferred habitats are wetlands and shallow lakes, where they swirl in circles sweeping their large bills back and forth on the surface of the water, bringing their food to the surface.

Both male and female are easily recognized by their shovel-shaped bills. Males are more colorful with their green heads and rufous flanks, while the females are mottled brown overall.

Gadwall

Anas strepera

L 20" | **WS** 33"

One of the most underappreciated species of waterfowl in the state, upon closer inspection, male Gadwalls are quite appealing. They are common throughout the year with the exception of summer, when only a handful can be found in the state mainly in the western Lake Erie basin marshes. Their numbers peak during spring (February-April) and fall (October-November), where they can be found on well-vegetated lakes, ponds, and wetlands. Males produce a frog-like *meep*, while females give a raspy *quack*. Groups of Gadwalls can be quite vocal as they actively feed on the surface of the water. In flight, the white secondaries are easily seen.

Male uniform gray with puffy head, black rump patch, and silvery tertials.

Females are very similar to female Mallards but have a puffier head with a steep forehead and a smaller, darker bill.

American Wigeon

Anas americana

L 20" | **WS** 33"

Found across Ohio, American Wigeons are most common during spring (late February to early April) and fall (October to November) during migration, where they inhabit ponds, marshes and occasionally farm fields. Smaller numbers remain in the state throughout the winter moving around to any open body of water. In the summer they become rare, but a few do remain, especially in the protected wetlands in the western Lake Erie basin. Known for their kleptoparasitism, they are the pirates of the waterfowl world occasionally chasing after other species for their food. Easily disturbed, they tend to flush sooner than other waterfowl, so they are best observed from a good distance. American Wigeons are more vocal than other ducks, with the males giving a distinctive three-part whistle regularly. Keep an eye out for the vagrant Eurasian Wigeon, which can occasionally be found in Ohio mixed with American Wigeons.

Males have a distinctive white forehead, green stripe behind the eye, and a small blue-gray bill.

The round head with black smudge around the eye and small blue-gray bill distinguishes the female from other species.

Northern Pintail

Anas acuta

L 20-30" | **WS** 35"

These elegant ducks are common throughout the state on lakes and wetlands, where they typically mix in with other dabbling ducks. Agile in the air and on the ground, they can sometimes be found walking in grain fields. The majority pass through Ohio from September to November in the fall and February to March in the spring. Over 3,000 have been recorded at Funk Bottoms Wildlife Area in the past. Hardier than other species, Northern Pintail regularly overwinter in all parts of Ohio, but are rarely seen during the summer.

Males are gray with a long slim neck, white breast and neck stripe, brown head, and long black pointed tail.

Females are less distinct but show a characteristically long neck along with a plain head and dark gray bill.

Mallard

Anas platyrhynchos

L 23" | **WS** 35"

The most familiar duck in North America, Mallards are common and widespread in Ohio occurring on virtually any body of water. A year-round resident, numbers increase during the winter, with the arrival of the Canadian population. Although it is tempting, feeding Mallards and other water-fowl bread crumbs in the winter can be harmful and should be avoided. A prolific breeder, Mallards seem to hybridize with just about any other duck. With the American Black Duck population in decline, these two are increasingly hybrid-izing, which creates confusion in identification. Mallards also commonly hybridize with domestic ducks, where many urban ponds and lakes host these ornamental birds. Females make the well-known duck *quack*, while the males produce a quieter, raspy call.

The green head, white neck ring, white outer tail feathers with curly black central feathers, and yellow bill are diagnostic for the male.

In flight, the bright green head of the male is conspicuous.

Females are tan-colored with white outer tail feathers, a royal blue speculum conspicuously bordered with white, and an orange bill marked with black.

American Black Duck

Anas rubripes

L 22" | **WS** 36"

Superficially seeming to be dark female Mallards, American
Black Ducks are dark brown causing them to appear "black"
from a distance. In Ohio they are most common from October to
March, while a small number remain in the Ohio over summer,
mainly along the Lake Erie basin. As a close relative of the
Mallard, American Black Ducks often mix with Mallards
on lakes, marshes, and ponds. They commonly hybridize as
well. Between 1966 and 2014, the American Black Duck
population declined 84 percent, but this trend appears to have
slowed since. In November 2000, nearly 15,000 were recorded
on Sandusky Bay.

Uniform brown, with paler head and
olive to yellow-green bill. In flight
the blue secondaries are all blue
with no white border as in Mallard.

Green-winged Teal

Anas crecca

L 14" | **WS** 22"

Our smallest dabbling duck, the Green-winged Teal is a compact duck that inhabits wetlands, ponds, small lakes, and even croplands. In Ohio we see their numbers peak during the spring (late February to April) and fall (September through November) migrations. Smaller numbers overwinter, and they are quite scarce in the summer. Fast and agile, they can take flight straight up from the water, while in the water they can dive for food or to avoid predators. Any wildlife area or refuge in the state are excellent places to see these, however Ottawa NWR has hosted thousands in the past. Males produce a clear whistle call, while the females give a series of piercing *quacks*.

Males have a rufous head with green streak behind eye, vertical white stripe on the side, and a buffy streak at the rear.

Females and non-breeding males are all brown overall with distinctive buffy streak at the rear.

Canvasback

Aythya valisineria

L 20" | **WS** 33"

The Canvasback is a large diving-duck preferring deep lakes, rivers, and marshes, where it dives underwater for food. Their unique head shape, long black bill, and flat forehead separate this species from the similar Redhead. In Ohio we start to see Canvasbacks in mid-October, with most departing the state by May, though a few stay the summer mainly in the western Lake Erie basin marshes. In Ohio, focus your search along the Lake Erie coastline and marshes, major rivers such as the Cuyahoga, Ohio, Maumee, and Great Miami, as well as large reservoirs. Canvasback are normally found in large groups and mixed with other diving-ducks such as Redhead, Ring-necked Ducks, and scaup. At least 9,000 were seen from Bay View on Sandusky Bay in 1997.

Males have a white body, black breast and bill, and a red head with flat sloping forehead.

A faded version of the male, females are best identified by the distinctive head shape with the flat sloping forehead and long bill.

Redhead

Aythya americana

L 19" | **WS** 29"

The Redhead is similar to the Canvasback, but easily told apart by its brighter red and rounded head, blue bill, and gray, as opposed to white, body. This diving duck occurs in much of the same areas as the Canvasback including Lake Erie, large reservoirs, and rivers, but tends to be more common with numbers in the hundreds and occasionally thousands. Redheads start to arrive in October and stay through the winter peaking between February and March, before departing by May. A very small number remain through the summer primarily in the northern and western part of the state. Females of this species rank first in waterfowl for brood parasitism, laying their eggs in other ducks' nests.

Males have bright red, rounded head, blue bill with a black tip, and a gray body.

Females are pale brown overall with a noticeably round head.

Greater Scaup

Aythya marila

L 15-22" | **WS** 30"

Greater Scaup is the larger of the two nearly identical scaup, but judging size in the field is not recommended in separating these common species. Greater Scaup tend to be more common along Lake Erie than inland but can turn up anywhere in the state, especially on larger reservoirs and rivers. Like other diving ducks, Greater Scaup occur in medium to large rafts and sometimes mix with other species, including Lesser Scaup. In flight, their wing stripe extends the full length of the wing; Lesser's fades halfway. Greater also tends to have a lower, rounded head. Greater Scaup arrive in Ohio around October and typically have departed the state by the end of April.

Male has a more rounded head with the peak at the front of its forehead. In flight the white wing stripe extends the full length of the wing.

Female is brown overall with a white patch behind the bill, best distinguished from female Lesser by head shape.

Lesser Scaup

Aythya affinis

L 16" | **WS** 29"

Like the very similar Greater Scaup, the Lesser Scaup occurs throughout the state on larger lakes and rivers but tends to be the more common scaup away from Lake Erie. They begin arriving in Ohio in the fall around mid-October and have normally departed by the end of April. A handful occasionally stay through the summer in Ohio, especially in the western Lake Erie basin marshes. Considerably more common than Greater, rafts reaching in the tens of thousands have been recorded on Lake Erie. The peak near the rear of the head and less white in the wings in flight help to separate this species from Greater Scaup.

Male very similar to Greater, but peak of head near the rear. In flight the white in the wing is less extensive than in Greater.

Female is nearly identical to the female Greater with brown coloration overall and white patch behind the bill. Best differentiated by head shape.

Ring-necked Duck

Aythya collaris

L 17" | **WS** 25"

This species deserves a name change, as the pale "ring" around its neck is hardly ever seen. "Ring-billed" Duck would better suit this duck, due to the obvious ring around the bill, which is characteristic of this species. In Ohio, Ring-necked Ducks begin to arrive in the fall around mid-October, with good numbers overwintering. During the spring their numbers peak from February to March before departing by mid-April. One or two individuals can occasionally be seen in Ohio during the summer but are not expected. They occur throughout the state on most bodies of water from rivers to wetlands and lakes.

Males have a black tail, back, neck and head with gray undersides, a peaked head, and a gray bill with a white ring and black tip.

Females are brown overall and similar to female scaup. Best distinguished by the paler head contrasting with a darker cap, a white ring around the eye, and a faint "spur" near the shoulder.

Surf Scoter
Melanitta perspicillata

L 21" | **WS** 30"

An uncommon migrant and winter resident, the Surf Scoter breeds in Canada and Alaska and passes through the Great Lakes on the way to the Atlantic Coast. In Ohio they are present from October to mid-May peaking in number between October and November. This is technically a sea duck, and your best chance of finding scoters is by scanning along the Lake Erie coastline, especially around Cleveland. Smaller numbers show up on larger lakes and rivers inland sometimes mixing with other species of scoters.

Male is black with white patches on the back of the head and forehead, a multicolored bill, and a white eye.

Female and immature dark overall with a white patch on the face and a second white vertical patch at the base of the bill.

Black Scoter

Melanitta americana

L 19" | **WS** 33"

The smallest and least abundant of the three scoters, Black Scoters are regular along Lake Erie and occasionally inland on larger lakes and rivers. Like the other scoters, they migrate through the Great Lakes in the spring and fall between their breeding grounds in Canada and the Atlantic Coast, where the majority spend the winter. The Cleveland lakefront is your best chance of finding this species, where they occasionally mix with the other species of scoters. Black Scoters are present in Ohio from October through April peaking in November.

Male entirely black with yellow knob on top of bill.

In flight, males are jet-black with obvious yellow knob on bill.

Female has dark brown body and pale cheeks contrasting with dark cap.

White-winged Scoter

Melanitta fusca

L 21" | **WS** 32"

The largest of the three scoters that passes through Ohio, the White-winged Scoter is one of the more likely scoter species to be found in the state. Breeders in Canadian freshwater lakes and ponds, they pass through the Great Lakes to the Atlantic Coast where they spend the winter. In Ohio they begin arriving in October typically along Lake Erie but can also be found inland on larger lakes and rivers. White-winged Scoters can be easily differentiated from the other two by the presence of a white wing patch, though this can sometimes be hidden at rest.

Adult male black with white wing patch and white "comma" below the eye. In flight, white wing patch is diagnostic.

Female and immature dark brown overall with white patches at the base of the bill and behind the eye. Watch for white wing patch to separate from female/immature Surf Scoter.

Long-tailed Duck
Clangula hyemalis

L 19" | **WS** 28"

This elegant species of sea duck breeds on the arctic tundra
of northern Canada and Alaska and winters on the ocean and
Great Lakes. Unfortunately, Lake Erie does not see the large
numbers that can be found on Lake Ontario, but we do see them
in small numbers every year. Fall migrants start to appear in
Ohio in late October primarily on Lake Erie but also on inland
reservoirs and rivers. From one to a dozen are typical, and they
all depart Ohio by mid-April. Good areas to search for Long-
tailed Ducks include anywhere along the Lake Erie coastline
from Lorain to Painesville as well as some reservoirs just south
of the lake, namely LaDue Reservoir and Mosquito Lake.

Adult winter male
is black and white
with long tail,
dark cheek patch,
and white crown.

Adult winter female has a
white face with a dark
patch behind its eye, dark
cap, mantle, and chest.

Bufflehead

Bucephala albeola

L 14" | **WS** 21"

The Bufflehead is North America's smallest species of water-fowl. These energetic ducks actively dive underwater for food at times making them difficult to get into your binoculars. At one moment you'll be watching one bobbing on the water and suddenly a dozen will appear. Occurring on deeper ponds, lakes, and rivers, Bufflehead begin to arrive in Ohio around late October and typically depart by the end of April. These cute little ducks with their disproportionately large heads and black-and-white patterns are unlikely to be confused with any other species.

Small and round headed, males have a white body, black and white head, and black back.

Females and immatures are brown overall with a distinctive oval white patch on the face.

Common Goldeneye

Bucephala clangula

L 18" | **WS** 31"

The stocky, black-and-white Common Goldeneye is a diving duck that can occur anywhere in Ohio. Fall migrants begin arriving in mid-October and will occupy large bodies of water. Flocks typically number around a few dozen but can reach the hundreds or even thousands, especially on Lake Erie. Most depart Ohio by the end of April for their Canadian breeding grounds. In flight, their wings produce a distinctive whistling sound, which is why hunters call this species the "whistler."

Male is black and white with dark tail, back, and head with distinctive white patch between the eye and bill.

Female has a gray body, brown head, yellow eye, and a dark bill with a yellow tip.

Hooded Merganser

Lophodytes cucullatus

L 18" | **WS** 24"

The smallest of the three mergansers that occur in the state, the striking Hooded Merganser is found year-round throughout Ohio. Fall migration picks up in mid-October and peaks in late-November where some rafts can be in the hundreds on larger reservoirs. LaDue Reservoir and Mosquito Lake are excellent places to see such numbers in the fall. During the winter, their numbers decrease but they will remain common on lakes, ponds, and rivers. Most of the wintering and spring migrants depart the state by mid-April, while some remain to breed. A cavity-nester, Hooded Mergansers breed in tree cavities and man-made duck boxes near forested wetlands.

The handsome male has a slender bill and an obvious large crest.

When crest is lowered, only a
white stripe is present.

Female, non-breeding male, and
immatures are dark gray and
brown overall with a lowered crest.

Common Merganser

Mergus merganser

L 25" | **WS** 34"

The large, stocky Common Merganser is found throughout Ohio on large lakes and rivers, where they dive underwater to catch fish. Most arrive in the state in November departing by mid-April. Numbers occasionally in the thousands can be seen feeding and migrating along Lake Erie. Although a rare breeder in the state, a few rivers in northeast Ohio host breeding pairs, including the Grand River and Little Beaver Creek, which are both designated Wild and Scenic by the Ohio Scenic Rivers Program. This says a lot about the importance of natural areas with limited human impact.

Male is long and sleek with a dark back and green head, which normally looks black in the field. The bright red bill is hard to miss.

Female clean gray overall with a rounded dark brown head and bright red bill. White patches under the throat and neck are quite contrasting.

Red-breasted Merganser

Mergus serrator

L 23" | **WS** 28"

The Red-breasted Merganser is most common in Ohio between October and May, where it is commonly found in groups on lakes and rivers. It is not uncommon to see hundreds and even thousands migrating along the Lake Erie shoreline. In November 2011, an astounding 197,000 were counted heading west off Rocky River Park near Cleveland. A few individuals are found lingering in most summers, mainly along Lake Erie. Like the Common Merganser, the Red-breasted Merganser has a serrated bill, which allows it to grip fish that it dives for underwater.

Male shaggy dark head, red bill, white neck, dark breast and back, and gray sides.

Female/non-breeding male gray overall with a prominent crested brown head. White on throat is not as contrasting as in female Common Merganser.

Ruddy Duck

Oxyura jamaicensis

L 15" | **WS** 23"

Compact and comical, the Ruddy Duck is known as a "stiff-tail" due to the wren-like tail that angles straight up. Occurring on wetlands, lakes, and reservoirs, Ruddy Ducks dive underwater to feed on invertebrates and occasionally plants. Although present year-round, they are most prevalent during the spring and fall migrations mainly from late October to early December and March through April. Smaller numbers remain over the winter where there is open water. Typically a breeder of the prairie pothole region of north-central U.S. and south-central Canada, a small number breed in the western Lake Erie marshes and occasionally inland.

Breeding male chestnut overall, black cap and nape, large white cheek and bright blue bill.

Non-breeding male like breeding male but brown instead of chestnut bodied. Blue bill not as bright.

Female is brown with a dark cap and dark line across the cheek.

Northern Bobwhite

Colinus virginianus

L 10"　|　**WS** 13"

Northern Bobwhite is the only native quail to the Eastern U.S. and is best known for its *bob-WHITE*! song. They were probably absent from Ohio before settlers cleared the extensive forests covering the state. With the increase in brushy wood edges, overgrown fence rows, old fields and pastures, bobwhites expanded north through Ohio eventually occurring in every county in the state. As a southern species, bobwhite numbers fluctuate from year to year with steep declines after harsh winters. The blizzard of January 1978 was particularly devastating to bobwhites, which resulted in a 90 percent decrease in numbers compared to the prior 17-year average. In addition, changes in farming practices which led to the removal of brushy woodlots and overgrown fencerows meant their numbers have not recovered. In Ohio the wild populations are mostly restricted to south-central and southwestern Ohio, though bobwhites are released all over the state as a popular game bird to hunt.

Male has black and white striped head and rufous breast band, while female (inset) has a more buffy face. Both sexes have ornately patterned brown and black backs.

Ring-necked Pheasant

Phasianus colchicus

L 24" | **WS** 22–34""

Native to Asia, Ring-necked Pheasants were introduced into Ohio in the 1890s for hunting. By the 1940s they had reached their peak of approximately five million birds in the state. Since then, their numbers have dropped considerably, with habitat loss and changing farming practices contributing to the decline. However, large numbers are still being released for sport including 14,000 in the fall of 2018 into 24 hunting areas. They occur throughout Ohio, mostly avoiding the southeastern part of the state, which lacks the preferred habitat of tall vegetation and overgrown fields in farming regions. Listen for the male's distinctive two-note *urrr-kik!*

Male is a large game bird with red facial skin, dark head with a white ring around the neck, various browns overall, and a long barred tail.

Female is light mottled brown overall with a long, pointed tail.

Ruffed Grouse

Bonasa umbellus

L 16-20" | **WS** 20-25"

The Ruffed Grouse occurs almost exclusively in the unglaci-ated regions of southern and eastern Ohio, where it prefers secondary forest cover. Due to Ohio's forests maturing and habitat loss, Ruffed Grouse numbers are at an all-time low within the state. These secretive gamebirds are difficult to see, but keep an ear out in the spring when males produce a drum-ming sound with their wings to attract a mate. From a distance it could sound like a motor starting, and if you're close enough you can even feel it in your chest. Most Ruffed Grouse in Ohio are the red color-morph, but the gray morph can occasionally be seen in northeastern Ohio.

A medium-sized crested game bird with elaborate gray or brown markings overall. Easily camouflaged.

Wild Turkey

Meleagris gallopavo

L 42" | **WS** 53"

Wild Turkeys were extirpated from Ohio by 1904, but reintroductions beginning in the 1950s were very successful. Turkeys now occur in all counties in the state, becoming more common in the south and eastern regions. Preferring a mixture of woodlands and agricultural fields, Wild Turkeys can also occur in urban areas with Cleveland having a well-established population. A "rafter" of Wild Turkeys are typically around 12-16 individuals sometimes detected by the male "gobble" or the high pitched *tuk tuk tuk* of the female. Watch for the males displaying by puffing their feathers, spreading their tail, and dropping their wings.

Very large game bird, dark brown overall, with unfeathered head. Male's head is covered with blue and red wattles.

In display males puff up, spread their tails, and drop their wings.

Pied-billed Grebe

Podilymbus podiceps

L 13" | **WS** 21"

The Pied-billed Grebe is a small waterbird occurring on lakes, ponds, and marshes throughout Ohio. Present year-round, their numbers peak during spring and fall migrations, particularly from March to May and September to October. During the summer they construct floating nests using vegetation that is anchored to emergent vegetation. Upon hatching, the young are known to leave the nest a day after fledging and spend much of the first week on their mother's back. Listen for their distinctive series of accelerating and decorating *clucks*.

Breeding adult tawny-brown, whitish bill with black band, black throat, and dark cap.

Non-breeding adult differs by lack of black on the cap, throat, and bill. Juvenile is like non-breeding adult but with zebra-striped face.

Horned Grebe

Podiceps auritus

L 14" **WS** 24"

A migrant and winter visitor, Horned Grebes are present in Ohio from late September through May most commonly along Lake Erie as well as inland lakes and rivers. Their numbers peak during the fall (Oct-Nov) and spring (Feb-Apr), when generally a dozen is a typical count. However, over a thousand have been recorded along Lake Erie near Cleveland in the past. Much of their time in Ohio they are in their drab black and white winter plumage; however, those lingering into April and May start to show their fresh breeding plumage. They tend to be silent in Ohio.

Breeding adult has a dark gray back, rufous flanks and neck, and a black head with two large yellow tufts.

Non-breeding adult has a gray-black back with gray underparts and a black cap sharply contrasting with a white face.

Red-necked Grebe

Podiceps grisegena

L 20" | **WS** 24-35"

This large and lanky grebe is an uncommon migrant in Ohio that is typically present from October to early December in the fall and from late February to early April in the spring, which is when they are more frequently seen. Preferring deeper water than other grebes, the Red-necked is generally found on Lake Erie and larger bodies of water inland. With its large size and long fairly heavy yellow bill, a Red-necked Grebe is unlikely to be confused with another species.

In breeding plumage, large with dark body, red neck, white cheeks, black cap, and yellow bill.

Winter adult and immatures large and dusky gray with paler cheeks and yellow bill.

Eared Grebe

Podiceps nigricollis

L 20" | **WS** 24–35"

Rare in Ohio, the Eared Grebe is a western species that regularly strays east into the state. They also occur throughout the Americas, Eurasia, and Africa. As a spring and fall migrant and winter visitor to Ohio, Eared Grebes are absent between June and August during their breeding season. They are similar to Horned Grebe, but keep an eye out for their head peaked at the front when scanning large lakes and reservoirs. The majority of birds in Ohio are in their non-breeding plumage with the exception of those in late spring when they have molted into their breeding plumage.

Breeding adult all dark with a black neck, wispy yellow plumes on its head, small black bill, and red eyes.

Non-breeding adult has a dark back and gray sides, neck, and bill. Dark cap spills down over face unlike the sharp contrast you see in Horned Grebes.

Rock Pigeon
Columba livia

L 13" | **WS** 23"

Introduced to North America in the early 1600s from Europe, the ubiquitous Rock Pigeon can be found practically anywhere in Ohio especially in cities, parks, and farmlands. Domesticated for racing, mail delivery, and pigeon collections, their colors can range from their natural gray to anything from brown, pied, white, or black. Nesting on buildings, bridges, and other man-made structures, their presence is sometimes given away by their low humming coos. When they take flight, they occasionally produce a slapping noise by clapping their wings together.

A plump pigeon with a white cere (a large, fleshy lump at the base of the upper bill). Most adults are pale gray overall with two black bars across their wings and a darker head.

In flight, most individuals have a dark tail band.

Others appear brown, pied, black, and white, among other colors. Large numbers congregate on rooftops, powerlines, and under bridges.

Eurasian Collared-Dove

Streptopelia decaocto

L 13" | **WS** 14"

A dove from the Indian subcontinent, this non-native species first reached the U.S. in the late 1970s in south Florida. They rapidly spread across the U.S., making it all the way to Alaska. Ohio was slow at picking up its first record only when a hunter shot one in Crawford County in 2001. Since then, their numbers grew gradually but haven't reached the prevalence of states to the west. Still, small numbers can be found in many small farming towns in the western half of the state, especially those with grain silos where food waste is prevalent. The towns of Celina, South Charleston, Vanlue, Sandusky, and Kidron are some of the more established places to find Eurasian Collared-Doves, and they are bound to become more widespread in the years to come. Listen for their repeated *koo-KOO-kook* song.

A fairy large all-gray dove with an obvious black ring on the neck. Extensive white undertail coverts visible on square tail perched and in flight.

Mourning Dove

Zenaida macroura

L 12" | **WS** 16"

Abundant and widespread, the Mourning Dove is a familiar species across Ohio. As the name suggests, their song is a mournful *hooOOOH ooh' ooh-oooh*, which some confuse with a distant owl. Present in a variety of habitats, they are readily seen perched on telephone wires and gladly feed on seed under bird feeders. Although they are not masters at nest building, sometimes throwing just a few small twigs together on a branch, they are successful breeders and often nest close to humans. Sleek and slender, the Mourning Dove is our only native dove in the state, after the Passenger Pigeon became extinct in the early 1900s.

Long slender dove with black spots on its wings and a long-pointed tail, which has white and black bands on the edge.

Yellow-billed Cuckoo

Coccyzus americanus

L 11" | **WS** 16"

More often heard than seen, Yellow-billed Cuckoos breed
throughout Ohio and prefer wooded corridors along streams
and rivers, second-growth forest, and even early second-growth
habitats. Listen for their throaty *ku ku ku ku ku kow kow
kowlp kowlp* or their slow repeated *kow kow kow kow kow*
calls. Generally a later migrant than many other birds, the
majority arrive or pass through on their way north from early to
mid-May to June. Watch for this sleuth species in tree canopies, where it specializes in eating caterpillars. Most will have
departed Ohio by the end of October.

Brown upperparts, white
underparts, mostly yellow
bill, and long black tail
feathers with white tips.

Black-billed Cuckoo

Coccyzus erythropthalmus

L 12" | **WS** 15"

Not as common in Ohio as the similar Yellow-billed Cuckoo, Black-billed Cuckoos are more often seen during spring migration from early May to early June. A scarce summer resident, small numbers breed throughout Ohio in second-growth forests, especially corridors along streams and occasionally aspen thickets in Ashtabula County. Higher concentrations breed in the northeastern corner of the state, while they are mostly scarce along the Indiana border. Listen for their staccato *tu-tu-tu tu-tu-tu tu-tu-tu* toots typically in series of threes.

Brown upperparts and pale underparts, mostly black bill, and brown tail with distinct small white tips.

Common Nighthawk

Chordeiles minor

L 9" | **WS** 22"

An iconic species over urban areas, Common Nighthawks are closely associated with Ohio's cities and towns, where they nest on flat gravel roofs between June and early August. Contrary to the name, they are not related to hawks, but instead form their own group also known as "goatsuckers" or "nightjars." Their appearance and flight suggest an oversized bat. The first spring migrants begin arriving in Ohio in late April with the majority moving through in May. At dusk watch the skies as dozens and even hundreds can migrate overhead and again in the fall from August to early October.

Slender, long tail and wings, white bars close to wingtips diagnostic.

Well camouflaged mottled brown, gray, black, and white. Small bill and extremely short legs. Note the conspicuous white patch on wing.

Chuck-will's-widow

Antrostomus carolinensis

L 12" | **WS** 24"

A master of disguise, a Chuck-will's-widow can go undetected sitting motionless in leaf litter or on a branch. Nearly the entire population in Ohio is restricted to the Ohio Brush Creek Valley in Adams County, with the Edge of Appalachia Preserve being your best chance of finding one. A nocturnal species, Chuck-will's-widows hunt at night by flying around with their beaks wide open catching insects in flight. To aid with this, they have prominent rictal bristles around the base of the bill, which help to funnel insects into their mouths. In order to maintain these specialized feathers, their middle toe is modified with a comb-like appendage used to preen these bristles. The species is typically recorded in Ohio between late April and early July. Listen for their *CHUCK-widow-WIDOW* song.

A large, flat-headed nightjar mottled buffy, brown and black.

Eastern Whip-poor-will

Antrostomus vociferus

L 10" | **WS** 19"

Cryptic and localized, the Eastern Whip-poor-will used to be more common throughout Ohio but has substantially declined during the twentieth century. Preferring brushy woodland edges and second-growth forest, much of their habitat either grew into mature woodlands or was converted to agriculture. Breeding mostly in the unglaciated southeastern region of Ohio, they begin arriving in the spring around April and can be quite vocal through May. A surprising number appear along the Lake Erie coastline during spring migration roosting directly on the ground in leaf litter or on a low branch. Listen for their *whip-poor-will whip-poor-will whip-poor-will* song. Edge of the Appalachia Preserve, Shawnee State Forest, and Lake Hope State Park are excellent places to listen for this species. Most will depart Ohio by the end of September.

Small nightjar with gray and brown camouflaged patterning. Males have large white tail corners visible in flight.

Chimney Swift

Chaetura pelagica

L 5" | **WS** 11"

Frequently called the "flying cigar with wings" after their body shape, Chimney Swifts are acrobatic insectivores that often feed over Ohio's cities and rural areas. A migrant and summer resident, swifts return to Ohio in April and depart by the end of October and are generally first detected by their distinctive chittering calls. They spend much of the time on the wing and prefer nesting in old chimneys. In the fall, large numbers assemble around large chimneys, especially on old schools, where they feed overhead. At dusk, they form impressive "tornadoes" of swifts funneling down into a chimney to roost for the night. Contact your local park district for information on public events to watch this spectacle, sometimes called "A Swift Night Out."

Dark brown, cigar-shaped body, long and narrow wings, and short tail.

Ruby-throated Hummingbird

Archilochus colubris

L 3" | **WS** 4"

Tiny and insect-like, the Ruby-throated Hummingbird is often mistaken for an insect such as a hawkmoth. Known for hovering, flying backwards, and even upside down, hummingbirds frequent wildflowers in woodlands and forest edges and are easily lured to backyard hummingbird feeders. Avoid using red dye or artificial hummingbird drinks; simply boil one-part white sugar and four-parts water. Ruby-throateds are common statewide from mid-April through mid-October but have been known to stay in Ohio as late as December. Any hummingbirds recorded from October onward should be scrutinized and photographed, as they could potentially be a vagrant species from the west, most likely a Rufous Hummingbird.

Male bright ruby-red throat, black mask, and green upperparts.

Female mostly white below with green upperparts. Lacks red throat.

Virginia Rail
Rallus limicola

L 9" | **WS** 14"

The elusive Virginia Rail prefers marshes with tall, dense cover and shallow water where it lurks for food out of view. In Ohio they are common and widespread with their greatest numbers along Lake Erie, where a lot of remnant marshes still exist. The removal of wetlands has caused a decline in numbers over the last century. Virginia Rails begin to arrive in April when they stake out their territories actively singing their *ti-dik-ti-dik-ti-dik* song at dawn and dusk. They will also give a series of loud grunt calls, which arouses a quick response by other individuals. Most depart Ohio by the end of October though a few will overwinter. Some reliable places to see and hear Virginia Rails include Spring Valley Wildlife Area, Battelle Darby Creek Metro Park, Killbuck Marsh Wildlife Area, Cuyahoga Valley National Park, and the western Lake Erie basin marshes, namely Magee Marsh and Mallard Club Marsh Wildlife Areas and Ottawa National Wildlife Refuge.

Adult cinnamon-colored overall with gray cheek, black-and-white barring on flanks, long red bill, and upright tail.

Sora

Porzana carolina

L 9" | **WS** 14"

Small and plump with a bright yellow bill, the Sora is more often seen in Ohio than our other rails, where it inhabits wetlands with cattails, rushes, and sedges. Although secretive, Soras are often seen feeding in the open flicking their tail, occasionally running back into cover when frightened. Rarely do they take flight. Around dawn and dusk, listen for their onomatopoeic song *sor-RA! sor-RA!*, which often ends with a descending whinny that lasts several seconds. Present in Ohio from April through October, rarely do they remain in the state any later.

Upperparts mottled brown and black with white edging. Gray neck gives way to barred white, brown, and black belly. Yellow bill sharply contrasts black face. Legs and feet also yellow.

Common Gallinule

Gallinula galeata

L 14" | **WS** 21"

Formally called the Common Moorhen, Common Gallinules favor marshes mixed with open water and dense emergent vegetation, where they nest under cover. Resembling a duck, gallinules are actually in the same family as rails but are generally much easier to see as they occasionally float in the open bobbing their heads along the way. Present in Ohio from late March through October, they are most common in the extensive marshes of the western Lake Erie basin including Magee Marsh and Metzger Marsh Wildlife Areas, Ottawa National Wildlife Refuge, and Howard Marsh Metro Park. Other areas that offer the best chance of seeing gallinules include Big Island and Killbuck Marsh Wildlife Areas, Mentor Marsh, and Battelle Darby Creek Metro Park. They normally announce their presence by their various whinnies, clucks, and yelps.

Medium-sized dark bird with yellow legs and toes, white markings on side and tail, red forehead shield, and red bill with a yellow tip.

American Coot

Fulica americana

L 16" | **WS** 24"

The American Coot can be found across Ohio on lakes, wetlands, and ponds, where it pecks at the water surface and dives for food. This species is not a duck, but a relative of rails and gallinules. The coot is unique in that it has lobed feet, which help it kick through water. Most coots are present in Ohio from October to May peaking during spring and fall migration, when groups of hundreds and even thousands are possible. During the summer, they become more uncommon with much of the population centered around the western Lake Erie basin and Sandusky Bay, while they become absent from the unglaciated region of the state. They give a variety of calls with an abrupt *krrp*! being the most common.

Dark gray to black overall with prominent white bill with a black ring at the tip.

Sandhill Crane

Antigone canadensis

L 47" | **WS** 79"

A state endangered species in Ohio due to habitat loss, Sandhill Cranes began nesting in Ohio in the mid-1980s after an absence of 60 years. Their numbers have slowly increased since then. In the spring and fall, watch the skies for large migrating flocks, sometimes numbering in the hundreds, as they fly overhead in V-formation. Note their extended necks and quick upward and slower downward wing beats when identifying.

In the summer, breeding pairs can be found in numerous wetlands and wet meadows in northern and central Ohio, where you may even see them perform their courtship dancing displays. Many of our breeding cranes will overwinter in Ohio, while others will head south for the winter. Big Island, Killdeer Plains, Funk Bottoms, Killbuck Marsh, Mosquito Creek, and Magee Marsh Wildlife Areas all offer an excellent opportunity of finding this regal species.

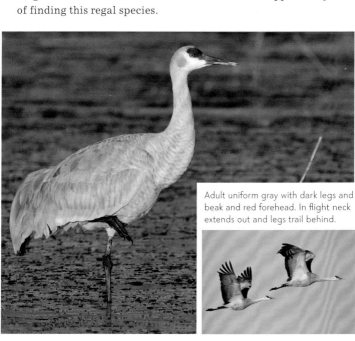

Adult uniform gray with dark legs and beak and red forehead. In flight neck extends out and legs trail behind.

Black-necked Stilt

Himantopus mexicanus

L 14" | **WS** 29"

More commonly found throughout the Western U.S., Gulf Coast, and Atlantic Coast, Black-necked Stilts have only recently expanded their range into Ohio. Still a rare migrant in the state, most pass through Ohio between April and May generally in the western half of the state. Black-necked Stilts prefer shallow wetlands and flooded agricultural fields, and have ended up breeding a few times, most notably at Howard Marsh Metro Park and Mercer Wildlife Area. With their long pink legs, they wade through the water searching for invertebrates and fish. When they are alarmed, listen for their repeated yipping call. All depart Ohio by the first week of September.

Adult black and white with pink legs and long black bill.

American Avocet

Recurvirostra americana

L 18" | **WS** 31"

The striking American Avocet with its elegant upturned bill is an uncommon migrant in Ohio. Preferring shallow wetlands, mudflats, and beaches, small numbers pass through Ohio in the spring (Apr-May) and fall (Jul-Oct), between their wintering and breeding grounds in the southern U.S. and the Great Plains respectively. Caesar Creek, Deer Creek, Buck Creek, and Alum Creek State Parks, the Conneaut sandspit, and the western Lake Erie basin wetlands host small numbers annually. In May 2015, an astounding flock of a hundred spent the day at Metzger Marsh Wildlife Area to the enjoyment of many birders. Watch for their unique feeding style as they sweep their bills back in forth in the water scything out aquatic invertebrates.

Adult black and white long-legged shorebird with a rusty head and neck and upturned bill.

Non-breeding like breeding adult without the rusty head and neck.

Black-bellied Plover
Pluvialis squatarola

L 11" | **WS** 24"

The largest plover in North America, the striking Black-bellied Plover passes through Ohio in the spring and fall between the wintering grounds in the southern U.S. and the breeding grounds on the arctic tundra in Canada and Alaska. Preferring mudflats, beaches, and tilled farmlands, a couple to a few hundred are possible during their peak migrations northward mainly in May and southward from August to October. Quite wary, Black-bellied Plovers are best viewed from a distance, and if disturbed they give a high whistled *pee-a-wee*. Mostly absent from south-central and southeastern Ohio, they are most often found along the Lake Erie coastline and beaches and mudflats of inland reservoirs.

Breeding male black belly, neck and face, short black bill, and mottled black and white back.

In flight, all ages show diagnostic black "armpits."

Non-breeding adults mottled brown and white overall. Stocky appearance with short black bill.

American Golden-Plover
Pluvialis dominica

L 10" | **WS** 22"

An extraordinary migrant, American Golden-Plovers winter in central and southern South America and breed in the high arctic tundra of northern Canada and Alaska undertaking one of the longest journeys of any shorebird. While the bulk of these plovers migrate through Indiana and Illinois, Ohio sees its fair share, especially in the western half of the state. During spring (Apr-May) and fall (late Jul to early Nov), watch for flocks sometimes numbering in the hundreds resting and feeding on open pastures and farm fields and occasionally on mudflats and beaches. Compare to the similar Black-bellied Plover, which lacks the gold coloration of this species. These two species can sometimes be seen mixed together for excellent comparison.

Breeding male has dark cap and white crown stripe extending down toward its shoulder sharply contrasting with the black face and underparts. Upperparts are mottled black, white, and gold. Breeding female a bit paler with brown cheeks.

Non-breeding adult and juvenile pale gray and brown overall. Barring on the underparts. Dark cap and white eyebrow.

Semipalmated Plover

Charadrius semipalmatus

L 7" | **WS** 15"

Our smallest plover, the Semipalmated Plover is a common
migrant in Ohio that peaks in the spring in May and in the fall
from mid-July through October. Breeding in northern Canada
and Alaska, very rarely do a handful stay in Ohio during the
summer as non-breeders. Visually similar to the Killdeer,
Semipalmated Plovers are smaller, have only one breast band as
opposed to two, and have a shorter bill. Watch for them on open
mudflats and beaches where they feed on aquatic invertebrates.
A sharp ear can occasionally pick out their *chu-wee* call which
make their presence known. When disturbed, they'll give a
harsh rapid *kip-kip-kip*.

Breeding adult brown upperparts, white
underparts, black breast band, crown
and eye patch, and black bill with an
orange base. Non-breeding (inset)
differs in having a brown crown, eye
patch and breast band (not black).

Piping Plover
Charadrius melodus

L 7" | **WS** 15"

The Piping Plover is a sandy beach specialist that blends in well with its environment. They occur in three distinct geographical breeding populations—the northern Great Plains, the Atlantic Coast, and the Great Lakes—and winter along the Gulf and south Atlantic Coasts. Due to human disturbance, predation, and loss of habitat, they are now listed as endangered under the Endangered Species Act. The Great Lakes population decreased from 500-800 pairs to only a dozen by the mid-1980s. Thanks to a dedicated effort, their numbers have increased in the Great Lakes to around seventy pairs in 2018, mainly in Michigan but also neighboring states and Ontario, Canada. After an eighty-year absence, Ohio saw a return with a pair breeding at Maumee Bay State Park in 2021. Elsewhere in the state, they remain a rare migrant along the Lake Erie coastline and very rarely inland during spring (Apr-May) and fall (Jul-Sep).

Small with a black collar and crown stripe, orange bill with black tip, often standing in a horizontal position.

Non-breeding adult pale gray collar, plain face and all black bill.

Killdeer

Charadrius vociferus

L 9" | **WS** 18"

The most ubiquitous of our shorebirds, Killdeer commonly nest statewide on bare ground in road verges, gravel driveways, farmlands, and even parking lots. Often detected by their namesake *kill-deer kill-deer* call. If you approach their nest too closely, they will feign a broken wing and lead you in the opposite direction. Common in Ohio from late February through November, they are regularly found even throughout the winter. During migration, they are often found on open mudflats.

Medium-sized plover with two black breast bands, brown upperparts, black forehead stripe, and a rufous tail visible in flight.

Will often feign a broken wing to distract intruders near its nest.

Upland Sandpiper

Bartramia longicauda

L 11-12" | **WS** 18-22"

Upland Sandpiper numbers in Ohio increased with the clearing of forests for farmland in Ohio during the nineteenth century, with breeding confirmations in all but ten counties. From the 1940s to 1970s, much of Ohio's grasslands were converted to croplands while hayfields were mowed more frequently. This resulted in a sharp decline in the historical range in Ohio. Upland Sandpipers are now listed as a state-endangered species and are breeding in only a handful of counties in the upper two-thirds of the state. As their name implies, they are not fond of mudflats in contrast to most shorebirds, but prefer prairies, grasslands, hayfields, and particularly the edges of small county airports. Migrants and breeders can be found in the state between April and September with a strong liking to perch on fence posts and telephone poles. Listen for their rising trill ending with a long descending whistle.

Tall and slender, long neck and small headed, speckled brown overall, with yellow legs and thin bill.

Whimbrel

Numenius phaeopus

L 17" | **WS** 33"

An uncommon to rare migrant in Ohio, the Whimbrel is a large shorebird with a characteristically long decurved bill. Favoring beaches along the Lake Erie coastline and occasionally inland reservoirs, most Whimbrels pass through the state between May and early June and again mainly from August to September. The Conneaut sandspit, Headlands Dunes State Nature Preserve, Lorain Harbor, and Maumee Bay State Park are some of the prime locations to try your luck at finding Whimbrels migrating along the lakefront and occasionally feeding on the shoreline. The third week of May is particularly a good time to find them. Listen for their loud repeated *whee-whee-whee-wheet-wheet*.

Large shorebird with a long neck and small head with a characteristically long curved bill. Note the striped crown and pale eyebrow.

Hudsonian Godwit

Limosa haemastica

L 14-17" | **WS** 27-29"

Godwits are characteristically large shorebirds with long straight or slightly upturned bills. The Hudsonian Godwit is a scarce migrant in Ohio with most occurring in the fall from August through early October, while very few move through in the spring. They typically occur as singletons or in small flocks. Keep an eye out for them along the Lake Erie shoreline where they may be found feeding on mudflats and marshes or flying offshore. Occasionally Hudsonian Godwits will appear inland on mudflats within wildlife areas or reservoirs. The western Lake Erie marshes offer your best chance at finding one of these infrequently recorded shorebirds.

Most birds present in Ohio are juvenile/non-breeding adults, which are grayish overall. More distinctive in flight with black "armpits" and white rump sharply contrasting with black tail tip. In May individuals will start to show reddish on the belly.

Marbled Godwit

Limosa fedoa

L 18" | **WS** 30"

One of the largest shorebirds to pass through Ohio, Marbled Godwits are uncommon spring (Apr-May) and fall (Jul-Oct) migrants between their wintering grounds along the Atlantic, Pacific, and Gulf Coasts and their breeding grounds in the northern Great Plains. Ohio sits well out of their migratory route, but a few individuals show up annually. Look out for them in shallow water where they feed almost exclusively on plant tubers during migration, contrary to most other shorebirds. Wetlands along the Lake Erie coastline offer your best chance of finding one, but inland wildlife areas and reservoirs can also play host to this species — especially Killdeer Plains Wildlife Area.

Large overall-buffy shorebird with unstreaked underparts, slightly upturned bicolored bill, and long legs. In flight lacks the black "armpits" and black-and-white tail of the Hudsonian Godwit.

Ruddy Turnstone

Arenaria interpres

L 9" | **WS** 21"

The Ruddy Turnstone is a beach specialist, turning over stones and debris in search of food—hence the name. One of the most widespread shorebirds in the world, in the U.S. Ruddy Turnstones winter along the coastlines and migrate to the high arctic for breeding. The Great Lakes are a favored stopover site to fuel up before continuing their spring and fall migrations. Most migrate through Ohio in May and again from mid-July to early October, where they mainly turn up along the Lake Erie coastline favoring sandy and rocky beaches. A smaller number will occasionally show up on beaches and mudflats on inland lakes and reservoirs. Aside from their distinctive and striking calico coloration, listen for their staccato rattle call.

Stocky with a short slightly upturned black bill, orange legs. Breeding birds have striking calico back and black-and-white face.

Juveniles and non-breeding adults brownish lacking striking orange, black, and white markings

Red Knot

Calidris canutus

L 10" | **WS** 21"

Red Knots undertake one of the longest migrations of any
bird, traveling from southern South America to their breeding
grounds on the high arctic tundra. The Great Lakes create an
ideal stopover location for them to refuel before continuing.
In Ohio, Red Knots are an uncommon migrant and are almost
always found along Lake Erie, though occasionally will show
up inland. Watch for these stocky shorebirds on mudflats and
beaches in May-June and August-October, where they typically
occur singly or a couple individuals. Due to a steady decline,
Red Knots are classified as near-threatened under the Endangered Species Act.

Medium-sized
chunky shorebird
with rich rufous
below and mottled
grayish above with
rufous edges.

Juveniles and
non-breeding adults
gray overall with
barring on the
flanks and chest.

Dunlin
Calidris alpina

L 7" | **WS** 15"

The hardy Dunlin is one of the first shorebirds to return to Ohio on their way north to their arctic tundra breeding grounds. Some will begin arriving as early as mid-March but will peak from mid-April to early June when hundreds or even thousands can be found foraging on mudflats. In flight, tight flocks will twist and turn in unison offering an impressive aerial show. A handful remain throughout the summer as non-breeders mainly at Ottawa National Wildlife Refuge, Howard Marsh Metro Park, and Metzger Marsh Wildlife Area in northwest Ohio. In the fall, the majority pass through between October and November with some individuals lingering as late as mid-January. Careful study of flocks may turn up the similar Curlew Sandpiper, a rare Eurasian vagrant to Ohio.

Stocky, medium-sized. Breeding plumage unmistakable with distinctive black belly and rusty back. Note long drooping black bill and black legs.

Typically in tight flocks, sometimes quite large. In breeding plumage, black bellies obvious.

Winter plumage uniform gray-brown overall. Short neck and long drooping bill diagnostic.

Sanderling
Calidris alba

L 8" | **WS** 15"

If you spot a small sandpiper chasing after receding waves only to high-tail it back on the next incoming wave and running around stopping only to feed, you probably found a Sanderling. These hyperactive shorebirds are most at home on beaches including the Lake Erie coastline and to a lesser extent inland beaches and mudflats. Wintering in temperate and tropical beaches worldwide, Sanderlings nest in the high arctic and pass through Ohio only in the spring (May to early Jun) and more frequently in the fall (Jul-Nov). Listen for their occasional "*wick*" call or twittering if in a group.

Plump with stout black bill, black legs, and no hind toe. Adult breeding plumage richly mottled rufous, black, and white on head, back, and breast. Clean white flanks and belly.

Juvenile similar to non-breeding plumage but with a checkered black-and-white back.

Non-breeding plumage pale gray above and white below with a dark shoulder bar.

Baird's Sandpiper

Calidris bairdii

L 7.5" | **WS** 15"

One of five small *Calidris* sandpipers known as "peeps,"
the Baird's Sandpiper is infrequent in Ohio. Along with
White-rumped Sandpiper, another *Calidris* "peep," these two
shorebirds appear elongated thanks to their long wings, which
extend well beyond their tail. Most of the Baird's Sandpiper
population migrates through the Great Plains between their
South American wintering grounds and their arctic tundra
breeding grounds; staying well west of Ohio. Virtually absent
in the spring, a small number are found every fall from late
July to early November throughout northern and western Ohio,
favoring the higher drier areas of mudflats and flooded fields.

Medium-sized and slender with buff
breast and scaly upperparts. Wing
tips extend well beyond tail. Black
legs and black somewhat droopy bil

White-rumped Sandpiper

Calidris fuscicollis

L 7" | **WS** 17"

A long-distance migrant, White-rumped Sandpipers are large "peeps" with long pointed wingtips that extend well beyond their tail. Visible only in flight, their rump is entirely white unlike our other small sandpipers. Similar in size to Baird's Sandpiper, White-rumped also favors drier areas of mudflats and wetlands but appears more robust with distinctive streaked flanks. Wintering in South America and breeding in the arctic tundra, small numbers of White-rumped Sandpipers pass through Ohio in the spring during May and early June. In the fall, their numbers increase slightly passing through from mid-July to early November peaking between August and September.

Medium-sized. Gray and rufous back, black legs, and streaking down the flanks. Base of lower-mandible is red-orange.

In winter plumage gray overall with faint streaking down the flanks, white supercilium, black legs, and red-orange at base of lower mandible.

Least Sandpiper

Calidris minutilla

L 6" | **WS** 11"

As the name implies, this "peep" is remarkably small, averaging
not much larger than a sparrow. In fact, Least Sandpipers
are the smallest shorebirds in the world. Common and widespread in the state during migration, in the spring we see their
peak numbers between late April through May on mudflats,
wetlands, and flooded fields, where they number from one
to a couple hundred. In June they are scarce, but late spring
migrants heading north and early returning fall migrants
heading south may overlap. Peak fall migration is between July
and October with singletons remaining in the state well into
winter. A vocal sandpiper, listen for its high-pitch *kreet* call.

Yellow legs diagnostic among
peeps, but mud can be deceiving.
Small decurved black bill. Adult
breeding has rufous and brown
speckling on back and heavily
streaked throat and breast.

Juvenile more colorful than adult with bright rufous, black, and white on the back and diffused streaking on throat and breast.

In winter white below and brownish above with smudged brown breast.

Western Sandpiper

Calidris mauri

L 6" | **WS** 12"

Often difficult to separate from the similar and more common
Semipalmated Sandpiper, Westerns have an obviously longer
bill with a less blunt tip. A scarce spring migrant during
May, the majority are found in Ohio in the fall from mid-June
through October, when they are still uncommon to rare. They
occur on open mudflats and shallow water often with flocks of
Semipalmated Sandpipers. Big Island Wildlife Area, Ottawa
National Wildlife Refuge, and Wilderness Road near Funk
Bottoms Wildlife Area regularly host Western Sandpipers.

Small peep with black legs
and long black bill which
droops slightly at the tip.
Rufous cap and cheeks with
rufous mottling on the back.

Juvenile brighter than most peeps, typically with a couple rows of rufous scapulars. Underparts clean white. Long bill with droopy tip is often distinctive.

Winter birds rather nondescript with white underparts and gray upperparts lacking any warm tones. Faint streaking on breast. Bill length diagnostic.

Semipalmated Sandpiper

Calidris pusilla

L 6" | **WS** 12"

The Semipalmated Sandpiper is one of the most common "peeps" that occurs in Ohio. A high-arctic breeder, Semipalmated Sandpipers breed in northern Alaska and Canada and winter along the coasts of Central and South America. In Ohio they pass through during the spring (late Apr to mid-Jun) and fall (early July through Oct), preferring open mudflats along Lake Erie and inland, and will occasionally turn up on beaches. As their name suggests, Semipalmated Sandpipers have small webbed toes unlike most of their cousins, but this feature is rarely seen in the field. Quite vocal; listen for their *chrrup* call.

Adult gray-brown and black above and pale below with faint streaking on breast. Bill is short, black, and noticeably blunt. Legs dark.

Juvenile like adult but scalier on back with more rufous and white edging to feathers. Darker cap contrasts with white eyebrow.

Pectoral Sandpiper

Calidris melanotos

L 9" | **WS** 17"

A medium-sized sandpiper with boldly striped brown breast sharply contrasting with white belly. Pectoral Sandpipers depart their South American wintering grounds in the spring, passing through Ohio between mid-March and May. On their artic breeding grounds, males inflate a throat sac which expands and retracts during aerial flight displays. Fall migration is drawn out from July through November. Pectoral Sandpipers prefer more vegetated mudflats, wetlands, and flooded farm fields than open mudflats. Quite vocal, listen for their distinctive *churk* call.

Medium-sized, moderately long head, heavily streaked brown chest contrasting with white belly, and yellowish or greenish legs.

Juvenile like adult but back scalier with more rufous edging.

Stilt Sandpiper

Calidris himantopus

L 8.5" | **WS** 16.5"

Between a dowitcher and a yellowlegs in size, Stilt Sandpipers can easily be overlooked when they are mixed in with
other shorebirds. Favoring mudflats and shallow pools, Stilt
Sandpipers feed in a typical sewing machine fashion probing
the mud, which causes them to blend well among dowitchers
and with their similar feeding habits. A rare spring migrant
in Ohio during May, we see the majority pass through in the
fall between July and October, when they are typically seen in
smaller numbers. Mostly absent from the Appalachian region of
southeastern Ohio, Stilt Sandpipers are regularly found along
Lake Erie and at inland wetlands and lakes. Big Island and
Killdeer Plains Wildlife Areas, Englewood Metro Park, Wilderness Road near Wooster, Berlin Reservoir, and the western
Lake Erie basin marshes are reliable fall locations to find Stilt
Sandpipers.

Medium-sized, long greenish
legs, slightly decurved bill.
Breeding plumage heavily barred
overall with rufous cheeks.

Non-breeding adults white
below, gray above, and a
prominent supercilium. Juvenile
similar but scalier on the back.

Buff-breasted Sandpiper

Calidris subruficollis

L 8" | **WS** 18"

This delicately beautiful shorebird winters on grasslands
in South America and breeds in the high arctic of Alaska
and Canada. Known for lekking, groups of breeding males
flutter-jump, raising one or both wings in the air as if waving
to attract a female. They'll even display to the occasional
human. In the spring, the population migrates north through
a narrow corridor in the Great Plains and rarely strays east.
Their fall migration is more widespread occurring in Ohio
but they remain rare. Watch for this species between August
and September (rarely October) on grass verges of mudflats
and wetlands, sod fields, and other short-grass habitats.
Typically found singly or in groups of up to five individuals,
larger numbers are occasionally reported in Ohio including an
astounding 76 in Ottawa County in 1985. Wilderness Road near
Wooster, Findley Reservoirs, the Conneaut sandspit, Ottawa
National Wildlife Refuge, and the "Lost Bridge" over the Great
Miami River west of Cincinnati have all been fairly reliable
every fall.

Medium-sized. Buffy face
and underparts and mottled
brown above. Head and bill
reminiscent of a dove.

Long-billed Dowitcher

Limnodromus scolopaceus

L 11.5" | **WS** 19"

Scarce in spring (late Feb to early May); very few individuals pass through Ohio typically earlier than the more common Short-billed Dowitcher. Any dowitcher present before April is likely Long-billed. In the fall, they remain uncommon, passing through from late July through November when they feed on invertebrates in shallow water and mudflats much like the Short-billed by rapidly stitching up and down like a sewing machine. Unlike Short-billed, Long-billed Dowitchers tend to have a more hunch-backed appearance compared to the Short-billed's flat back, and are generally more vocal including a high-pitched *keek* often heard in flight.

Medium-sized shorebird with obvious long bill. Breeding adult gorgeous with rufous face, neck, breast, and belly with dark spotting becoming more barred near the flanks. Rufous edging to black back feathers.

Juvenile less colorful than adult with mostly gray wings and rufous edging to back feathers.

Winter adult like Short-billed—gray overall. Best told by shape and voice.

Short-billed Dowitcher
Limnodromus griseus

L 11" | **WS** 19"

The Short-billed Dowitcher is far more common in Ohio than its Long-billed Dowitcher counterpart. Feeding in shallow water or mudflats and sandy beaches, they typically associate in small to large flocks and occasionally associate with other larger shorebirds, including yellowlegs. They are easily separated from other shorebirds by their feeding pattern of rapidly stitching up and down much like a sewing machine while they feed on invertebrates in the mud. Their northward migration in Ohio begins in April, peaking in May, and rapidly dissipating by early June. In the fall, the majority of Short-billed Dowitchers pass through the state from July to October. In flight, their white rump patch is obvious. They will sometimes give a low-pitched *tu-tu-tu* call, unlike that of the Long-billed Dowitcher.

Medium-sized shorebird with long bill twice the length of the head. When feeding, back appears flat. Breeding adult buffy on face, neck, breast and belly. Supercilium contrasts sharply with dark cap. Lightly spotted on breast and sides becoming more barred on the flanks. Legs dull yellowish and bill dull greenish becoming darker near the tip. Bill length generally shorter than Long-billed Dowitcher but plenty of overlap.

Winter adult pale gray overall with all other features similar to breeding adult.

Feeding pattern is rapid stitching up in down in the mud under water, much like a sowing machine.

American Woodcock

Scolopax minor

L 11" | **WS** 18"

Known as a "Timberdoodle" to some, the American Woodcock
is a plump, comical shorebird of woodland edges. Common
across Ohio, they are among the first migrants to return to
the state and will arrive as early as February. Throughout the
spring woodcocks preform a "sky dance" much to the delight
of birders. From a clearing on the ground, they give several
amusing *peent!* calls (compare to Common Nighthawk) before
flying straight up into the sky. This is followed by an amazing
flight display 200-350 feet up of twists and turns before zigzagging back to the ground while whistling a *cheap-chip-chirp,
cheap-chip-chirp* with their modified wing feathers. Well
camouflaged in leaf litter, woodcocks feed on earthworms
by probing their long bill into the soil. Eyes set far back on
its head give this bird excellent rearview binocular vision to
help detect predators. By November most will have left the
state, though a small number will overwinter, especially
during mild winters.

Chubby; buffy orange
below and black and gray
above blending surprisingly
well in leaf litter. Nearly
tailless and neckless, eyes
and bill exceptionally large.
Note the black barring
across the crown.

Wilson's Snipe

Gallinago delicata

L 12"   **WS** 17"

The cryptic Wilson's Snipe blends well in its environs, which include wetlands, flooded fields, grassy meadows, and mudflats. Present year round in Ohio, they are most common during spring migration from late February to early May and again during fall migration from July through November. A smaller number remains throughout the state all winter, showing up on a good number of Christmas Bird Counts. As a scarce breeder in Ohio, they are less often seen in the middle of summer. With luck, however, you may witness their aerial display which involves an eerie winnowing call. Throughout the year flushed birds will give an abrupt *crate!* call as they rapidly zig-zag away from you.

Medium-sized chubby shorebird intricately patterned brown, black, and white. Three long buffy streaks down the back are usually visible. Short legs and long bill.

Wilson's Phalarope

Phalaropus tricolor

L 9" | **WS** 15-17"

The Wilson's Phalarope is the largest and most regular of the three species of phalaropes but remains uncommon. Present in Ohio from late April through October, most pass through during the spring and fall. A breeder of interior lakes in the western U.S., a few will remain in Ohio through the summer, but very rarely do they breed. Unlike most other birds, phalaropes are known for their reversed sex-role mating structure. Females are the highly ornamented individuals who compete for mates, while the males take care of all parental care. Watch for them in marshes as they spin in circles on the water pulling up crustaceans and insects to feed on. Rarely do they coinhabit with other shorebirds on open mudflats.

Breeding female colorful with a blue-gray and chestnut back, gray cap, black strip through the face and down the neck with a peachy border. Bill thin and straight. Legs black. Male like female but much duller.

Juvenile more intermediate between breeding and non-breeding adults. Dark cap, white neck and belly, and yellow legs. Back variably scaly from rusty to grayish.

Non-breeding adult gray overall with a white neck and belly. Legs yellow unlike breeding adult.

Red-necked Phalarope

Phalaropus lobatus

L 7.5" | **WS** 15"

The Red-necked Phalarope is one of the smallest shorebirds in the world and spends much of its life at sea off the Pacific coast of South America. In the spring they migrate north to their arctic breeding grounds and are scarce migrants in Ohio during May. In the fall, they are uncommon in the state between August and October. Like other phalaropes, watch for them on marshes and other shallow bodies of water where they will spin in circles pulling up invertebrates to eat. Phalaropes are known for their reversed sex-role mating system, with the females the more brightly plumaged individuals. The Lake Erie lakefront offers your best chance of finding a phalarope, especially the western basin, but any pond or inland wetland may play host to a phalarope in the spring and fall.

Breeding female (pictured) gray overall with white belly, bright rufous neck stripe, and white chin. Bill straight, thin, and black. Male (not pictured) a duller version of the female.

Juvenile like non-breeding adult but with gold stripes on the back.

Non-breeding adult white overall with gray and black mottled back, a black cap, and black stripe through the eye.

Spotted Sandpiper
Actitis macularius

L 8" | **WS** 15"

The most widespread breeding shorebird in North America, the Spotted Sandpiper is common in Ohio from April through October along the Lake Erie coastline and inland bodies of water. Their numbers peak during the spring (late Apr to May) and fall (late Jul to early Sep). The Spotted Sandpiper is well known for its constant teetering and when they take flight, they give a *peet-weet* call with a flight characterized by quick bursts of shallow wingbeats followed by a glide. Unlike other shore-birds, Spotted Sandpipers generally remain singly or in small groups and rarely in the larger numbers of other species. "Spotties," as they are affectionately known, are always a welcome sight for birders.

Short pinkish yellow legs and short neck; in flight, wings show a white wing stripe. Breeding adult characterized by white undersides, brown upperparts with distinctive black spotting on neck and flanks.

Juvenile very similar to
non-breeding adult but note
boldly patterned upper wing
coverts and a generally very
clean and fresh plumage.

Non-breeding adult like
adult but lacks the
spotting, but instead has
brown sides of breasts.

Solitary Sandpiper

Tringa solitaria

L 8" | **WS** 17"

The Solitary Sandpiper winters in the tropics and breeds in
the boreal forest of Canada and Alaska, where it is one of the
very few species of shorebirds that breed in trees. Most migrate
through Ohio between April and May and July to October where
they can be found singly or in small numbers in wet or muddy
habitats such as lakes, ponds, flooded farm fields, and mudflats.
As their name implies, they rarely appear in groups of substantial numbers. When flushed or flying over, Solitary Sandpipers
give a *wheet-wheet-wheet* call like Spotted Sandpiper but more
evenly pitched.

Brown back with small white
spots, obvious white eye ring,
white belly, and yellow-green leg
Compare to Lesser Yellowlegs.

Willet
Tringa semipalmata

L 15" | **WS** 28"

When standing out on a mudflat with other shorebirds, Willets are very nondescript, chunky shorebirds. When they take flight, their bold white wing stripe says otherwise. Willets are uncommon migrants in Ohio with most sightings involving one or a small handful of individuals. High counts are occasionally reported in the 50s and on rare occurrences over 100. Inland records appear throughout the state mainly along shorelines of large lakes and wetlands. The Willet gets its name due to its ringing call *pill-will-willet*. Present from late April through early November, the majority pass through the state between late April and early May and from July to early September. Anywhere along the Lake Erie shoreline offers your best chance at finding this scarce migrant, as well as in some productive inland areas that host good shorebird numbers.

arge stocky shorebird with long legs and thick straight
ill. Upperparts mottled and underparts intricately barred.

n flight, bold black-and-white wing pattern diagnostic.

Greater Yellowlegs

Tringa melanoleuca

L 12" | **WS** 24"

This leggy shorebird is a common migrant in Ohio during spring and fall on mudflats, shallow marshes, and flooded farm fields. One of the first shorebirds to arrive in Ohio in the spring, start looking for them in March though the majority pass through between April and May. Not as abundant as their smaller counterpart, the Lesser Yellowlegs, often these two species mix together allowing easier differentiating between the two. Both have obvious yellow legs, but Greater is larger, longer billed, and gives a *tew-tew-tew* call in sequences of three or more instead of two. In the fall, Greater Yellowlegs pass through between July and November.

Medium-sized lanky shorebird with long yellow legs, bill twice the length of the head, olive-gray upperparts, and streaked neck and breast.

Lesser Yellowlegs

Tringa flavipes

L 9" | **WS** 24"

Slim and delicate, the Lesser Yellowlegs is a common migrant across Ohio favoring mudflats, shallow marshes, and flooded farm fields, where they will occasionally wade into the water in search of food. Very similar to its larger counterpart, the Greater Yellowlegs, the Lesser is smaller, shorter-legged, smaller-billed, and gives a *tew-tew* call typically in sequences of two. When both species are not standing side-by-side, judging size might not be straightforward. Mirroring Greater Yellowlegs, Lesser Yellowlegs migrate through Ohio from late March through May and again from July to November. A very small number of non-breeding individuals may be present in mid-summer.

Long yellow legs, olive-gray upperparts, white underparts with streaked neck and breast. Bill length roughly the same width as the head. In flight white rump obvious with black barring on tail.

Bonaparte's Gull

Chroicocephalus philadelphia

L 13" | **WS** 31"

This small tern-like gull is common on lakes and rivers across Ohio and can be seen any month of the year. In spring, dazzling adults with their full black hoods move north through the state. In the fall, their numbers swell with impressive concentrations from late October to early December along Lake Erie numbering in the thousands and occasionally tens of thousands. These large numbers are always worth scanning for rare species such as Little Gull and Black-headed Gull. The annual winter kill-off of gizzard shad in sometimes-frozen Lake Erie probably aids in attaining these concentrations. The *grr grr* call of the Bonaparte's Gull very much resembles a small tern's call.

Small gull with thin black bill and red legs. Breeding adults have an entirely black hood with thin white crescents around the eyes

In flight, adults have an all-white tail, white leading edge to wings, and black tips to the primaries.

In winter, black hood is replaced with a black smudge behind the eye; legs pink.

Herring Gull
Larus argentatus

L 24" | **WS** 56"

Common and widespread, Herring Gulls occur in much of the
same areas as the more plentiful Ring-billed Gull from lakes
to rivers, landfills, and farm fields. Present year-round in Ohio,
Herring Gulls are most abundant during the winter where
greater concentrations can be found on larger reservoirs, rivers,
and particularly Lake Erie. During the summer, they are more
restricted to Lake Erie where they nest on islands and flat rooftops as well as in larger inland cities and reservoirs. Herring
Gulls take four years to reach adult plumage, with countless
variable plumages in between resulting in much confusion.

Large gull with pale eyes,
pink legs, and yellow bill
with a red dot on the lower
mandible. Adult breeding
has clean white face, neck
and underparts, and pale
gray back and wings.

Juvenile uniform brown with mottled brown and white back. Unlike adults, eyes and bill entirely black.

Non-breeding adult like breeding adult but has extensive brown streaking on face and neck.

Ring-billed Gull

Larus delawarensis

L 19" | **WS** 44"

A medium-sized gull, Ring-billed Gulls are common in Ohio and occur on lakes, rivers, farm fields, landfills, and notoriously in fast food restaurant parking lots. Their abundance and urban existence make these gulls your typical "seagull." During the winter months, their numbers swell, with counts of 100,000 or more recorded along Lake Erie where they take a liking to gizzard shad. Their numbers drop during the summer and will mainly occur in larger cities, reservoirs, and Lake Erie where they will breed in noisy colonies. As their name suggests, all but juvenile Ring-billed Gulls have an obvious black ring around their bill. Their calls are the typical loud, raucous calls that gulls are known for.

Medium-sized gull with yellow bill with a black ring and pale eyes. Adults in breeding plumage have clean white head, neck, and underparts, a light gray mantle, and black wingtips lined with white spots. Legs bright yellow. Non-breeding individuals similar to breeding adults but have dark streaking on the head and neck.

Juvenile mottled brown overall with mostly dark bill. Immature variable depending on age, ranging from dark barring on neck and flanks, dark coverts, and pink bill with a black tip to more adult-like appearance, although retaining a dark tail band.

Glaucous Gull

Larus hyperboreus

L 27" | **WS** 59-71"

This large pale gull is exceeded in size only by the Great Black-backed Gull. Breeding along the Arctic Ocean of far northern Alaska and Canada, a small number make it as far south as the Great Lakes during the winter. In Ohio we see singletons and occasionally double digits between November and April mainly along Lake Erie. Anywhere along the Cleveland lakefront where gull numbers are concentrated during the winter could host one or more Glaucous Gulls. The more the weather replicates the arctic, the better. Inland they are rare, occasionally showing up on larger rivers, lakes, reservoirs, and of course landfills. Mostly white, all plumages lack any black in the wingtips.

Large and bulky. Adult pale gray above, entirely white elsewhere including unmarked wingtips. Bill and eyes yellow. Legs pink. Told from similar Iceland Gull by size, bulkiness, and larger bill.

Juveniles and immatures mostly white with a variable amount of pale brown markings. Long bill bicolored with dark tip.

Iceland Gull

Larus glaucoides

L 21-24" | **WS** 45-58"

The Iceland Gull nests on rocky ledges and sea cliffs in Greenland and the Canadian Arctic. In winter they move south reaching the Great Lakes but remain uncommon to rare in Ohio between November and April. Variable in size and plumage, larger adults with darker mantles are from the western populations formerly treated as a separate species called "Thayer's Gull." These can be difficult to differentiate from Herring Gull. Some Iceland Gulls are white overall, resembling the larger Glaucous Gull. Anywhere along the Cleveland lakefront offers your best chance at finding this winter resident as well as harbors that host large concentrations of gulls including Huron, Lorain, and Fairport Harbors.

Paler adult light gray above with white primaries frequently with gray tips, rarely black. "Cute" appearance thanks to small yellow bill and round pigeon-like head.

Immatures often pale to tan resembling Glaucous Gull but smaller in size with smaller bill. Bill varies from all black in younger birds to pink with a black tip in older immatures.

Darker adult, formerly "Thayer's Gull," resembles Herring Gull with slightly darker mantle, smaller bill, and rounded head often heavily streaked. In flight the wing tips are mostly white from below with limited black from above.

Lesser Black-backed Gull

Larus fuscus

L 23" | **WS** 56"

An Old World species, Lesser Black-backed Gull numbers increased on the northeast coast of the U.S. eventually expanding into the Great Lakes by the early 1980s. In Ohio they are now rare to locally common and continue to increase in numbers. This dark-mantled gull is most readily found along the Lake Erie coastline between September and March often mixed with Herring Gulls, though they can be present any time of year. As they become more widespread, inland records are becoming more prevalent. Over half of the inland counties have records, with plenty of inland reservoirs and landfills having a small number present every winter. This species is likely to continue increasing and is becoming more widespread throughout the state. Halfway in size between the smaller Ring-billed and larger Herring Gull, Lesser Black-backed Gulls have darker mantles, but not quite as dark as the much larger Great Black-backed Gull.

Adult dark gray mantled, yellow legs and bill, and long wings. Breeding adult has a clean white head and neck while non-breeding adult has dense streaking, especially around the eye.

Juvenile with dark mottling on back and streaked breast differentiated from Herring by pale head, which is shared by Great Black-backed Gull. Told apart from Great Black-backed by smaller size, longer wings, and less robust bill.

Great Black-backed Gull

Larus marinus

L 30" | **WS** 60"

As the largest species of gull in the world, with a very
dark mantle, this gull stands out like a sore thumb. Great
Black-backed Gulls breed along the Atlantic Coast of the
northeastern U.S. north through the Canadian maritime provinces and winter further south along the coast and throughout
the Great Lakes. In Ohio they are present year-round but
remain rare in the summer, where a few decide to stay south
and not breed. During the winter, numbers can reach into the
hundreds along Lake Erie, where they are most common. Inland
records are uncommon to rare, mostly in the northern tier of the
state where they sometimes frequent larger lakes and reservoirs
and landfills.

Large and bulky with a fierce look. Adults
have little to no streaking on an
otherwise clean white head, neck, and
underparts. Wings and back very dark
and primaries black with large white
spots. Robust yellow bill and pink legs.

Immature has a mostly white head, faint markings on
neck and flanks, checkered back and robust two-tone bill.
Juvenile like immature but underparts, neck, and head
more heavily streaked, and bill all black.

Black Tern

Chlidonias niger

L 9" | **WS** 23"

An attractive dark tern with a buoyant zigzagging flight, the
Black Tern is an uncommon migrant and rare summer resident
favoring lakes, rivers, and wetlands. In the summer, most breed
in the western Lake Erie basin of Ottawa, Lucas, Sandusky, and
Erie Counties where their preferred nesting habitat of freshwater marshes with emergent vegetation is present. Howard
Marsh Metro Park, Metzger Marsh Wildlife Area, and Ottawa
National Wildlife Refuge have all been traditional sites to see
this species. Over the years their numbers decreased mainly due
to wetland loss across their breeding range and decline of their
food because of agricultural control for insects and overfishing
along their winter range of Central and South American coasts.
They are now listed as a state endangered species in Ohio. Most
arrive in Ohio in late April and normally have departed by early
October.

Breeding plumage head, neck
and body black, wings and
back gray, and vent white.

Flight is characterized by a buoyant butterfly-like flight. Tail is only ever-so-slightly notched.

Non-breeding plumage, most of the black is gone remaining only on top of the head extending behind the eye.

Common Tern

Sterna hirundo

L 14" | **WS** 30"

Common Terns used to be more common in Ohio and nested in great numbers along the western Lake Erie basin. A combination of habitat loss, predation, and competition with the increasing number of nesting gulls, breeding Common Tern numbers decreased enough to land them on the state endangered list for Ohio. Now they nest only on a handful of islands as well as on artificial nesting platforms such as at Cedar Point National Wildlife Refuge (Lucas County) and Willow Point Wildlife Area (Erie County). During migration however, they are common to uncommon migrants throughout the state, showing up on lakes, reservoirs, and rivers from April through November. Similar to Forster's Tern, Common Terns are told apart during breeding season by their gray bellies (opposed to white) and non-breeding birds by their dark hindcrown and black carpal bars on the wings. A musical two-syllabled *keeyurr* is typically heard as they fly over.

Adult breeding plumage gray overall with paler cheeks, black cap, and red-orange bill with a dark tip. Tail typically shorter than wingtips.

In flight, upper wing uniform gray, unlike Forster's.

Non-breeding individuals like breeding adults but white underparts, white forehead, and dark carpal-bar.

Forster's Tern

Sterna forsteri

L 13" | **WS** 31"

Forster's Tern is a common migrant in Ohio and typically more abundant than the similar Common Tern. They are present from April to November with an obvious reduction in numbers during the mid-summer (June-July), when non-breeders may persist. Found throughout Ohio on larger lakes, rivers, and Lake Erie, their *jeer* call is similar to Common Tern but lower-pitched. Forster's Terns are best told apart from adult breeding Common Terns by their all-white underparts and longer tail projection, and from non-breeding adults by having a dark mask, not cap, and lack of dark carpal bar on the wings.

Adult breeding underparts all-white contrasting with pale gray wings and back. Full black cap, orange bill with black tip, and tail projection usually extending beyond the wings.

In flight, white contrasting primaries diagnostic. Deeply forked tail.

Non-breeding adults have a dark mask, not a cap, and an all-black bill.

Caspian Tern
Hydroprogne caspia

L 20" | **WS** 50"

Roughly the size of a Ring-billed Gull, the Caspian Tern is the largest tern in the world and has a global presence on all continents with the exception of Antarctica. They are present throughout Ohio from April through October on Lake Erie and inland lakes, reservoirs, and rivers. Although they breed on the Great Lakes, Ohio has no nesting records even though they are present throughout the summer. In late summer, adults are joined by juveniles which remain dependent on their parents. With their large size, big red bill, and harsh *rau rau* and *rapreau* calls, it's hard to mistake this species.

Large size and bright red bill diagnostic. Overall white with pale gray wings and back, black cap, and black legs. In flight, tail only slightly notched.

Red-throated Loon

Gavia stellata

L 24" | **WS** 43"

The Red-throated Loon has a circumpolar distribution breeding on remote ponds in the high arctic tundra. The smallest member of its family, Red-throated Loons are scarce migrants and winter visitors to Ohio, occurring on large lakes, reservoirs, and Lake Erie as they migrate between the Atlantic Coast and their northern breeding grounds. Unlike other loons, Red-throated Loons are rather slim. Often, they hold their thin bill tilted upward. Your best chance of finding one is by searching along the Lake Erie waterfront from late October through April between Sandusky and the Pennsylvania border as they tend to avoid the shallow western basin. Inland, Findley Reservoirs, LaDue Reservoir, and Englewood Metro Park seem to play host almost annually among other productive lakes.

Nearly all found in Ohio are non-breeding adults with the red throat absent. White face, neck, and underparts. Dark upperparts with white speckling. Thin bill typically pointed upward.

Common Loon
Gavia immer

L 26-36" | **WS** 41-52"

The mournful cries of the Common Loon are well known to those who have spent summers on backcountry lakes in the northern U.S. and Canada. In Ohio they remain silent but are common migrants in the spring from March to May and in the fall between October and December. During mild winters, when lakes remain ice-free, a small number may persist. Large and stocky, Common Loons sit low in the water, occasionally diving for food for long periods of time. In flight, they look stretched out with their feet extending as long as their neck and head. A lake watch along Lake Erie during mid-fall may produce hundreds of Common Loons migrating offshore.

Large waterbird with heavy bill, checkered back, and distinctive black-and-white striped collar. Sits low in the water.

Non-breeding adult and immature lack sharp contrasting field marks, but a pale collar is usually visible.

Double-crested Cormorant

Phalacrocorax auritus

L 32" | **WS** 47"

With the banning of DDT and other harmful pesticides, Double-crested Cormorant numbers have increased dramatically in Ohio. After an absence of breeding in over a century, colonies sprung up in the 1990s, and today cormorants are now common breeders in Ohio, especially in the western Lake Erie basin. West Sister Island hosts the largest colony of this gregarious species. Found throughout the state year-round, they are most common from spring through fall along Lake Erie, inland lakes and reservoirs, and large rivers, where they dive underwater for fish. Mostly silent, cormorants produce croaks and grunts, especially at breeding colonies.

Adult black with orange skin at base of long thin bill. Often seen with wings spread open to dry.

Immature like adult but gray-white neck and breast.

American White Pelican
Pelecanus erythrorhynchos

L 62" | **WS** 108"

The American White Pelican is an uncommon migrant, though their numbers are increasing annually in Ohio and nationwide. The decrease in PCBs and mercury pollution in the Great Lakes certainly helps. Most sightings within the state occur during the spring (Apr-May) and fall (Sep-Oct) mainly in the western Lake Erie basin. However, American White Pelicans have shown up throughout the year along Lake Erie and inland lakes and rivers. With their large size, massive yellow-orange bill, and nine-foot wingspan, they are hard to miss. With their increasing presence, perhaps one day they will start nesting in the state on offshore islands in Lake Erie.

Very large white waterbird with massive yellow bill. Breeding adults develop a plate on the upper bill.

In flight, all white with black flight feathers. Graceful flier, usually in small groups.

American Bittern

Botaurus lentiginosus

L 24-33" | **WS** 39"

One of Ohio's most cryptic species, the medium-sized American Bittern blends in perfectly with its densely vegetated wetland habitat. A scarce migrant and rare breeder from March through November, during migration American Bitterns can turn up in any wetland in the state. Breeders, however, are restricted to a few regions, most notably the western Lake Erie basin and northeastern Ohio. A crepuscular species, listen for their bizarre liquid calls, *unk-a-chunk, unk-a-chunk* and if you're lucky, one may take flight and drop into another section of wetland providing some extended flight views. Wetland loss resulted in a major decline of American Bitterns across the United States, landing them on the Ohio state endangered list.

Well camouflaged medium-sized heron with long thick neck and bill. Brown overall with pale stripes.

Least Bittern

Ixobrychus exilis

L 13" | **WS** 17"

The smallest heron in North America, the Least Bittern can be tough to see as it skulks through dense emergent wetlands, especially where thick stands of cattails are present. Your chances of finding one of these state-threatened species increases at night when they tend to vocalize, giving a cuckoo-like call. Present in Ohio from mid-April to mid-October, some reliable sites to try your luck include Mallard Club Marsh, Metzger Marsh, and Pipe Creek Wildlife Areas in northwestern Ohio, Mentor Marsh in northeastern Ohio, and Battelle Derby Creek Metro Park in central Ohio.

Small and compact. Crown and back dark green, neck, underparts brown and white, and wings chestnut. Highly contrasting pale lines border the scapular feathers. Bill yellow and long; eyes bright yellow.

Great Blue Heron

Ardea herodias

L 38-54" | **WS** 66-79"

Standing nearly four feet tall, often quietly along ponds and rivers, Great Blue Herons are ubiquitous throughout Ohio. Their diet consists mostly of fish, but they are also known to take a variety of other prey including amphibians, reptiles, birds, insects, and small mammals. In Ohio, Great Blue Herons are present year-round, but their numbers decrease in winter. During the breeding season (late-Mar to June), Great Blue Herons nest in colonies known as heronries. Some popular heronries worth visiting can be found at Pickerington Ponds, Lake Hope, Winton Woods, The Rookery (Geauga County), Cowan Lake State Park, and Cuyahoga Valley National Park. Often confused with a crane, Great Blue Herons keep their necks curled in s-formation, not fully extended as in cranes. Mostly silent, they will often give a harsh croak when flushed or disturbed.

Large, long-legged heron, grayish-blue overall, white head with a wide black strip extending from above the eye to the back of the head. In flight, dark legs extend beyond the tail.

Great Egret
Ardea alba

L 39" | **WS** 54"

With their hefty size, all-white plumage, black legs, and yellow bill, Great Egrets stand out like a sore thumb. Occurring in wetlands, rivers, ditches, and flooded fields, Great Egrets will feed on a variety of prey including insects, fish, frogs, snakes, crayfish, and insects. Nearly hunted to extinction in the late 1800s for their plumes, their numbers increased rapidly with protection during the twentieth century. The Great Egret is the symbol of the National Audubon Society, which was created in-part to protect herons and egrets from plume hunters. In Ohio, they can show up anywhere around the state from late March through November, with the majority occurring in the western Lake Erie basin. As with other species in their family, Great Egrets nest in colonies known as rookeries. West Sister Island NWR in western Lake Erie hosts the largest breeding colony in the Great Lakes.

Tall, pure-white egret, with all-black legs and yellow bill. Much larger than Snowy Egret, which has yellow feet. In flight, entirely white with legs extending well beyond the tail and neck curled in.

Snowy Egret

Egretta thula

L 24" | **WS** 39"

A medium-sized all-white egret, Snowy Egrets have yellow feet and a mostly black bill, which distinguish it from the larger Great Egret. Their spectacular head plumes were once highly coveted for women's hats in the 1800s, costing more than their weight in gold. Their numbers have rebounded since being protected, and they are now widespread but uncommon in Ohio. Present in the state from mid-April to October, they are mostly found in the western Lake Erie basin, but do turn up at wetlands and reservoirs around Cincinnati, Dayton, and Columbus regularly. A state-endangered species, Snowy Egrets now nest on West Sister Island in Lake Erie.

Medium-sized, all-white plumage, black legs with distinctive yellow feet, and black bill with a yellow base. Feeds more actively than Great Egret, often running after prey in the water.

Yellow-crowned Night-Heron
Nyctanassa violacea

L 24" | **WS** 42"

The Yellow-crowned Night-Heron is a scarce summer visitor and extremely rare breeder in Ohio, which is at the northern edge of the range. Preferring shallow, rocky streams and rivers, Yellow-crowned Night-Herons specialize in eating crustaceans, especially crayfish, staying true to their southern Cajun habits. Roosting concealed during the day, as other night-herons do, Yellow-crowneds also hunts at night. There are probably more breeding locations yet to be discovered in the state due to the difficulty of finding them. Only a handful have nested in Ohio in recent times, mainly in Columbus and Dayton. The most famous breeders in Ohio were the individuals that nested annually in sycamores over a road in the Bexley neighborhood of Columbus. After entertaining hundreds of birders for decades, these individuals have not been reported since 2015. The species is present in Ohio from April through September

Compact and gray, with a thick neck and blocky head. Adult has boldly black and white patterned head with a yellow crown. Juvenile (inset) brown with streaking overall and tiny white spots on wings and back. Similar to juvenile Black-crowned, note the robust black bill.

Black-crowned Night-Heron

Nycticorax nycticorax

L 24" | **WS** 46"

Black-crowned Night-Herons are a state-listed threatened species in Ohio despite their worldwide occurrence. Habitat loss, harmful pesticides such as DDT, and polluted water all contributed to their decline. Although they can be found statewide all year long, breeding occurs only on a couple of islands on Lake Erie—most notably West Sister Island, which holds 40 percent of all breeding herons and egrets within the Great Lakes. During the day, night-herons hunch motionless in trees over water until dusk when they head to their feeding areas, often giving their *wok* call in flight. The majority depart Ohio for the winter. Researchers have tracked most going to Florida, although one traveled all the way to Guatemala. Urban rivers such as the Cuyahoga River in Cleveland and the Scioto and Olentangy Rivers in Columbus host healthy overwintering Black-crowned Night-Heron populations.

Medium-sized stocky heron with shorter legs than Yellow-crowned. Body gray and white with a black cap and back, yellow bill, and red eyes. Juvenile (inset) brown with large white spots on wings and back, and white streaks on neck and underparts. Bill pale yellow.

Green Heron

Butorides virescens

L 17" | **WS** 26"

Green Herons are solitary birds often found feeding inconspicuously along quiet ponds and rivers. Small and compact, Green Herons are gray-green with a black crown, back, and wings, chestnut neck, and yellow legs. Most begin arriving in Ohio in April and are common summer residents statewide. As skillful hunters, Green Herons will use a "lure" for fishing. Tossing an object such as a feather into the water within striking distance, when prey comes to investigate, the heron will extend its neck at great speed snatching up a fish, insect, or other prey item. When disturbed, Green Herons will emit a loud distinctive *keow,* which typically gives away its presence. Most depart the state by the end of October.

Adult small and compact and gray-green. Neck is chestnut with white streaks down the throat. Bill is blac and legs bright yellow. Immature similar but with pale speckling on wings.

Osprey
Pandion haliaetus

L 22" | **WS** 59–71"

The Osprey is a real success story in Ohio. Persecution and habitat destruction combined with widespread use of chemicals such as DDT led to plunging numbers. After a reintroduction program in the mid 1990s, Ospreys are now breeding at just about every large lake and reservoir in the state. They feed primarily on fish by hovering over water, plunge-diving, and taking flight with their catch. A summer resident only, Ospreys begin arriving in the state in March and are best detected by their high-pitched whistling. Sticks on a human-made wooden platform structure over water are a tell-tale sign of a breeding pair, though they will occasionally nest elsewhere including on the top of cell towers. Most depart from the state by early November.

Large, brown above, white below with a white head and distinctive broad brown line through the eye. Beak is black and sharply hooked. In flight (inset), white belly contrasts with strongly barred wing feathers and brown "wrists."

Black Vulture

Coragyps atratus

L 25" | **WS** 57"

In the last century, Black Vultures have expanded northward and now occur throughout Ohio though they remain uncommon to rare in the northeastern and northwestern corners. As with Turkey Vultures, they are primarily scavengers, but they are also known to take calves and other young livestock, leading some livestock producers to consider them pests. Black Vultures tend to be social, sharing roosts and having strong long-term pair bonds. With a less developed sense of smell, Black Vultures can't find carrion by smell alone. Instead, they follow Turkey Vultures to food and ultimately displace them. Black Vultures are best told apart from Turkey Vultures by their gray (not red) head, shorter tail, horizontally held wings, more active wing flapping, and white patch under the primaries. Lacking a syrinx, or voice organ, Black Vultures are limited to producing hisses and grunts.

Large, black body, and black bald head. Pale legs.

In flight, broad wings, shor head and tail, pale wing tips sharply contrasting against black wings.

Turkey Vulture
Cathartes aura

L 28" | **WS** 69"

A familiar sight over rural and urban habitats, Turkey Vultures have a strong sense of smell, which helps them find carrion from up to a mile away. They aid in keeping our roadways clear of dead animals. Although present in the southern tier of the state year-round, they are common statewide from late February through November and are easily told by their characteristic v-shaped wing dihedral as they glide above the tree line in search of food. Their red head appears bald but does contain many small feathers, which help to keep the head clean when they probe into the guts of dead animals to feed. But don't get too close to inspect a vulture, because it will project vomit as a defense against predators. Mistakenly called "buzzards," our vultures are not related to the hawks named buzzards in Europe. Generally silent, Turkey Vultures will occasionally hiss.

Large and black with brown mottling on wings, red mostly featherless head, pale legs, hunched posture.

Large, dark, soaring raptor with little wing flapping. Black body, contrasting with gray wing feathers and red head, is diagnostic.

Northern Harrier
Circus hudsonius

L 19" | **WS** 43"

Northern Harriers are often seen flying low over grasslands and marshes, taking rodents and birds among other prey by surprise. With their long tail, wings held in V-formation, and white rump patch, Northern Harriers are one of the more distinctive raptors in Ohio. Common statewide during the winter and migration, Northern Harriers have become scarce breeders due to the decline in health of Ohio's grasslands since human colonization. Where they do breed, they nest directly on the ground typically in dense clumps of vegetation. The north-western Ohio marshes, the southeastern Ohio reclaimed strip mines, and the central Ohio Amish communities are some areas with higher concentrations of this elegant raptor. Mostly silent, they will occasionally give a loud shrill whistle.

Medium-sized with broad wings, long tail, and diagnostic white rump patch. Adult male gray above with black trailing edge to wings.

Immature like female but chest cinnamon brown and lacking the streaking.

Adult female brown above and heavily streaked brown below. White rump patch diagnostic.

Sharp-shinned Hawk
Accipiter striatus

L 10" | **WS** 17–27"

Roughly the size of a Blue Jay, the Sharp-shinned Hawk is one of Ohio's smallest raptors. They are most common during spring and fall migration (Apr-May; Sep-Oct), when they can turn up just about anywhere. During the summer, they breed mainly in the more forested southern and eastern regions of the state. Most migrate out of Ohio for the winter. This feisty pint-sized predator feeds mainly on birds and will occasionally be seen raiding bird feeders for a quick meal. Sharp-shinned Hawks are best distinguished from the similar Cooper's Hawk by their smaller size, smaller head, and squared tail tip. They are frequently detected by their high-pitched, agitated *kik-kik-kik* calls.

Adult blue-gray above, pale below with horizontal orange barring across breast. Head proportionately small compared to body. Tail long.

Immature brown above and heavily streaked below.

In flight, short rounded wings are frequently pushed forward. Tail tip squared, unlike rounded in Cooper's.

Cooper's Hawk

Accipiter cooperii

L 17" | **WS** 25-36"

Cooper's Hawks are well adapted to urban and suburban environments, where bird feeders provide easy access to their main prey: birds. Favoring woodlands, Cooper's Hawks, with their short rounded wings, are very agile at flying through the canopies of trees and taking birds by surprise. Now common, this wasn't always the case. Cooper's Hawks were severely affected by the use of DDT, but have made a strong comeback after this insecticide was banned. More regularly seen in Ohio than the similar Sharp-shinned Hawks, Cooper's Hawks are slightly larger, about the size of a crow, have a noticeably large head, and a rounded tail tip in contrast to the Sharp-shinned's square tip. These stealthy raptors are typically quiet but will give a loud *cak cak cak* call near their nest.

Adult blue-gray above, pale below with orange barring across the breast. Head proportionately larger than Sharp-shinned Hawk, and with a dark cap. Tail very long.

In flight relatively short, rounded wings and long tailed, which is rounded at the tip. Head projects well beyond the wings, not often seen in Sharp-shinned.

Immature brown above and heavily brown streaked below. Same upright posture as adult with larger head and long tail.

Bald Eagle

Haliaeetus leucocephalus

L 28-38"　|　**WS** 80"

Every American knows the Bald Eagle, our national emblem since 1782. Once abundant across North America, persecution from humans and insecticides including DDT greatly reduced their numbers, landing them on the Federal Endangered Species List in 1978. The following year there were only four nests in all of Ohio. With state and federal protections, as well as exceptional work from wildlife biologists and concerned public, they are no longer on the endangered list. As of 2018, there were 286 nests in Ohio. They are now found in every county in the state, with the greatest concentration in the western Lake Erie basin region at Magee Marsh Wildlife Area, Pickerel Creek Wildlife Area, and Ottawa National Wildlife Refuge, as well as Mosquito Lake in northeastern Ohio, and Killdeer Plains Wildlife Area. They are also found in urban environments including a pair in downtown Columbus along the Scioto River. Their call is a laughing *ki-ki-ki-ki-ki* cry.

Takes five years to reach adult plumage. Immature mottled dark brown with variable amount of white in the wings.

Adult massive, all dark-brown with obvious white head and tail.

In flight large broad wings held in a flat plane. Wing beats slow and powerful.

Red-shouldered Hawk
Buteo lineatus

L 20" | **WS** 40"

Red-shouldered Hawks were once the most common hawk in Ohio until the early to mid-1900s when much of Ohio's mature forests, their preferred habitat, were logged. The use of insecticides such as DDT increased their decline. With Ohio's forests maturing once again and the banning of DDT, Red-shouldered numbers are on an upsurge. Along with mature forests, particularly in moist lowlands, they are at home in well-forested suburban neighborhoods and often frequent backyards. In Ohio they are most common across the southern forest regions and the northeast, with growing numbers in areas like Columbus and the Oak Openings Preserve near Toledo. They are often detected by their distinctive *kee-ah kee-ah* cries.

Medium-sized hawk. Adult reddish barred underneath a■ darker upperparts with white spotting. In flight wings and t■ are barred black and white.

Immature lacks reddish barrin■ Upperparts are brown with w■ spotting. Underparts white w■ dark-brown vertical streaking■

Broad-winged Hawk

Buteo platypterus

L 15" | **WS** 35"

Our smallest buteo, the Broad-winged Hawk is an uncommon summer resident, mainly in the unglaciated region of southeastern Ohio where large tracts of mature upland forests are present. They may also be seen elsewhere in the state, especially in the northeastern and southwestern corners. During spring (Apr/May) and fall (Sep) kettles of dozens and occasionally hundreds can be seen migrating overhead between their breeding grounds and Central and South American wintering grounds. A forest specialist, they feed mainly on birds, insects and reptiles. Aside from their small size, they are easily told apart from other hawks by their three alternating black and white stripes on their tail. A long thin whistle sometimes gives their presence away, a call that doesn't make you think of a hawk initially.

Immature brown above and white below with broad brown barring on breast. Tail has many narrow bands.

Small hawk. Adult brown above with a variable amount of brown barring below. Tail is distinctively marked with broad black and white bands.

Rough-legged Hawk

Buteo lagopus

L 20" | **WS** 53"

A winter visitor to Ohio, Rough-legged Hawks are present in the state from November to early April in open habitats including grasslands, agricultural fields, and marshes. Like kestrels, they will hover in flight looking for small mammals and birds, before plunging down to catch their prey. They will perch on fences, utility poles, and often on a small branch at the top of a tree, where they seem too heavy for the support of the twig. Two color variations, or morphs, occur in this species: light and dark. Both variations can be seen in Ohio with the light morph being more common. An artic-nesting raptor, its feathering extends all the way down the legs, resembling a hare's foot, which acts as warm leggings for perching in snow.

Narrow wings and longish tail. Adult light morph has black wrists and black edging to wings and tail. Mottling on wings and amount of black on belly variable, with females having less mottling but more black on the belly.

Immature light morph mostly white head, tail, and wings; obvious black belly, black wrists, and black wing tips.

Adult dark morph two-tone underneath with black body contrasting with pale flight feathers.

Red-tailed Hawk

Buteo jamaicensis

L 22" | **WS** 49"

The most common and widely distributed hawk in North America, the Red-tailed Hawk is the most frequently seen raptor in Ohio all year round. Red-tailed Hawks can be found in a variety of habitats including agricultural lands, grasslands, open woodlands, and even urban environments. They have a strong fondness for perching in trees along roads and highways where they hunt for rodents, hares, and snakes along the open verges. Adults have a diagnostic red tail, but immature birds do not. Ohio occasionally hosts leucistic or albino individuals that are regularly mistaken for Snowy Owls, but the owl's shape, head size, and season help distinguish it from the hawk. The Red-tails' call, a far-carrying *kee-eeerr!* is commonly heard when they are circling overhead.

Adult mostly pale below with dark edging to wings and tail. Variable amount of black markings on belly. Tail noticeably red. Immature (inset) lacks red tail, instead barred brown and white.

Barn Owl

Tyto alba

L 14" | **WS** 44"

Barn Owls require vast open grasslands to hunt. With changes
in agricultural practices and land use, their numbers have
declined. They are categorized as threatened on the Ohio
Division of Wildlife list. The largest population in the state is
centered in the Amish communities in Wayne and Holmes counties, where farming practices haven't modernized and residents
place nesting boxes in their barns. Elsewhere in the state, there
are smaller numbers mainly in south-central and eastern Ohio.
The Ohio DNR Division of Wildlife has identified key areas to
encourage breeding. During the winter of 2018, the Division
placed more than 120 new Barn Owl boxes, working mostly
with private landowners, in the hope that the owls' numbers
will increase in the state. Unlike other owls that hoot, the Barn
Owl makes a loud, harsh scream lasting several seconds.

Medium-sized with
heart-shaped white
face. Richly colored
brown and gray on back
and mostly white below
with small black spots.

Eastern Screech-Owl

Megascops asio

L 8" | **WS** 22"

Our smallest and most common owl in Ohio, the Eastern
Screech-Owl ranges throughout the eastern deciduous forests
of the U.S. and southern Canada. In Ohio they are found in all
counties year-round occupying woodlands, shady residential
areas, urban parks, and cemeteries with large trees. Strictly
nocturnal, they hunt at night when they feed on an impressive
variety of prey items including rodents, birds, insects, and even
fish. During the day, they can be found roosting in a hollow tree
or a nest box, even boxes placed for Wood Ducks. There are two
color morphs: gray and rufous. In southern Ohio, the morphs
are evenly mixed, but as you go north, gray morph birds become
more common. Contrary to their name, they don't necessarily
screech but instead whistle either a monotone trill or a drawn-
out quavering whinny, which can easily be imitated by a human.
Pairs will occasionally call together with the male's call being
the lower-pitched.

Rufous morph is bright
reddish brown with dark
streaks and barring below

mall with short ear tufts.
dult gray morph is gray
verall with dark streaks
nd barring. When
wake, eyes yellow.

Great Horned Owl

Bubo virginianus

L 22" | **WS** 40–57"

Large, powerful, and widespread, the Great Horned Owl is the second most common owl in Ohio after the Eastern Screech-Owl. Favoring a mix of woodland, open fields, and marshes, Great Horned Owls feed on larger prey items such as rabbits and rats, but have been known to take skunks, cats, and even young Ospreys from their nest. The Magee Marsh Wildlife Area and surrounding locations have several active nests observed by thousands of birders who travel there every year for spring migration. Listen for their call after dusk, a loud series of hoots *whoo-whoo-whoooo-who-whoo*.

Very large owl with large ear tufts and yellow eyes. Heavily barred and mottled throughout with a white throat.

Snowy Owl

Bubo scandiacus

L 24" | **WS** 54"

Snowy Owls breed in the Arctic and during the winter are rare visitors to Ohio. In search of prey, only one or two may appear in some winters, while in other years dozens are possible. Few will venture farther south into the state and are accidental away from Lake Erie. Snowy Owls are most often seen on breakwalls, harbors, and airports—all open environments that resemble their breeding grounds up north. Unlike other owls, Snowy Owls tend to be diurnal doing much of their hunting during the day. If Lake Erie freezes along the shoreline, some individuals may hang out at the edge of the ice shelf hunting ducks for several days. They are most often present from mid-November through February, though some individuals have stayed as late as May and even June.

arge owls with various amount of dark barring. Adult male early all white with very little to no barring. Adult female as some dark barring throughout except on face. Immature emale (inset) has the most barring, excluding the face and nderwings. Eyes yellow.

Barred Owl

Strix varia

L 19" | **WS** 41"

A common to fairly common resident in mature woodlands statewide, the Barred Owl is best known for its call, which sounds like *who cooks for you, who cooks for you all*. Closest in size to the Great Horned Owl, Barreds lack ear tufts and have dark eyes and an obvious facial disk. Nesting takes place in early spring in large cavities of mature trees. Preferring small rodents such as moles and voles, Barred Owls will also eat a variety of other prey including amphibians and fish. Primarily nocturnal, Barred Owls are most active at night, especially after dusk, but this doesn't stop them from calling midday on cloudy days. Head to your nearest mature woodlands and listen after dusk, and you just may find yourself a Barred Owl.

Fairly large with rounded head, black eyes and yellow bill. Note the lack of ear tufts. Dark horizontal streaks across chest and vertical streaks on belly.

Long-eared Owl

Asio otus

L 15" | **WS** 36"

Long-eared Owls are uncommon to rare migrants and winter visitors to Ohio from the boreal forests of Canada and the northern U.S. During the day Long-eared Owls roost communally with a strong liking to pine plantations, but will also roost in dense grape tangles. Most are recorded in northern and western Ohio. Long-eareds have nested in a couple of dozen counties in the northern tier of the state, but not often in recent years. Perhaps similar to Great Horned Owl in appearance, Long-eared Owls are much smaller and slimmer. When threatened, they stand erect and compress their bodies amazingly thin. If you observe this in person, you're likely too close and should back away slowly.

Long and slender with orange facial disc, yellow eyes, and very large ear tufts.

Short-eared Owl
Asio flammeus

L 15" | **WS** 37"

A very rare breeder in Ohio, Short-eared Owls are the only species of owl in the state that builds its own nest, a shallow depression on the ground lined with down feathers and grasses. In winter, they are more common especially in open grasslands and marshes where meadow voles, their preferred prey, are bountiful. When hunting, their deep wingbeats are very distinctive and are described as having a moth-like flight. A diurnal species, short-eareds hunt mostly during the evening before dark. As the name suggests, they indeed have ear tufts, but these are often not visible due to their small size. Some areas worth checking for this species include The Wilds, Battelle Darby Creek Metro Park, Huffman Prairie, Killdeer Plains, Magee Marsh, and Wilderness Road near Wooster.

Moth-like flight, usually observed just before sunset. Barred wingtips.

Medium-sized heavily streaked owl with a whitish face and dark patches around yellow eyes. Small ear tufts difficult to see.

Northern Saw-whet Owl

Aegolius acadicus

L 8" | **WS** 17"

Undoubtedly our cutest owl, the Northern Saw-whet Owl is roughly the size of a robin and passes through Ohio each spring and fall. With their stealthy habit of roosting in conifers, grape tangles, and shrubby thickets, they are one of the hardest species of owls for birders to find. Widespread banding operations in Ohio and neighboring states and provinces revealed that saw-whets are far more common than previously thought. Formerly rare breeders in Ohio, they are no longer known to breed in the state. Very few overwinter, preferring states to our south. Although they rarely call in Ohio, they give a series of extended monotonous piping whistles.

Tiny owl with rounded head lacking ear tufts. Mostly brown above and pale below with brown vertical streaks. Note white "eyebrows."

Belted Kingfisher

Megaceryle alcyon

L 13" | **WS** 21"

A loud rattling call often alerts you to the presence of a Belted Kingfisher. With their massive bill and large crest, these birds are rarely confused with anything else. Belted Kingfishers occur along streams, rivers, ponds, and lakes, anywhere small fish occur. From a perch or hovering in flight, kingfishers will detect a fish in the water and dive bill-first to catch it. They will proceed to a nearby perch and whack the fish repeatedly, stunning or killing it before tossing it up in the air and swallowing it whole. They are indeed the king of fishing. Aside from fish, they will also eat crayfish, tadpoles, and frogs. Belted Kingfishers tend to be solitary except during breeding season (Apr-Jul) when they actively and aggressively defend their female and territory from other males.

Medium-sized stocky bird with large head, crest and bill. Blue-gray head, back, and breast band. Female has a chestnut belly band and flanks. Male lacks chestnut belly band and flanks.

Yellow-bellied Sapsucker

Sphyrapicus varius

L 8" | **WS** 15"

Aside from their silly name, Yellow-bellied Sapsuckers are well known for maintaining sap wells in the bark of trees for food. These shallow holes, generally in numerous rows, are attended daily to ensure sap flow. Yellow-bellied Sapsuckers are most common during spring (Mar-May) and fall (late Sep-Oct) migration, when they occur statewide in backyards, cemeteries, woodlands, and parks. During the winter, they remain fairly common but in the summer they are restricted to the far north-eastern corner of the state in Ashtabula, Trumbull, Geauga, and Lake counties where a small population breeds. In this region, they prefer aspen thickets on the edge of bogs and wet beech woodlands. Listen for their squealing *quee-ah* call and like other sapsuckers from the western U.S., their irregular drumming which starts fast and slowly tapers off.

Adult male has red crown and throat, white to yellowish underparts, and mostly black wings with white vertical wing patches. Female similar but lacks red throat. Juvenile (below) lacks red crown and throat and is browner.

Red-headed Woodpecker

Melanerpes erythrocephalus

L 8-9" | **WS** 16-17"

Once abundant in Ohio, numbers of the striking Red-headed
Woodpecker have declined in the state as much as 78 percent.
Causes include competition with the non-native European
Starling, logging, removal of dead trees, and urbanization.
Present year-round in oak-hickory woodlands, forest edge,
open country with scattered large trees, parks, and especially
golf courses, Red-headed Woodpeckers are most common from
May to September. This species will nest in tree cavities as well
as in utility poles and wooden fences. Known for caching food,
Red-headed Woodpeckers will store acorns and other nuts in
trees for the winter. With a variety of calls, drums, and chirps,
Red-headed Woodpeckers mainly give a gruff *tchur* call, like
Red-bellied Woodpeckers but higher pitched.

Bright red head and large bill. Back and
wings black with white wing patches. Belly is
clean white. Young birds have a brown head
instead of red.

Immature has grayish head, mottled back,
and black barring across white wing
patches.

Red-bellied Woodpecker

Melanerpes carolinus

L 9" **WS** 15"

Conspicuous and noisy, the Red-bellied Woodpecker is a
common species throughout Ohio. Occurring in a variety of
deciduous habitats, these medium-sized woodpeckers can be
found in mature and second-growth forests, woodlots, backyards, parks, and cemeteries and are very common visitors to
birdfeeders, especially with suet. As their name suggests, they
have a wash of red on their lower belly, but this can be chal-
lenging to see. With their zebra-striped wings and back and
red crown and nape, they are not likely to be confused with our
other woodpeckers. Red-bellied Woodpeckers are quite vocal
giving either a rolling *kwirr* or a coughing *cha-cha-cha*.

Zebra-patterned back with
pale underparts. Hint of red
on belly only occasionally
seen. Adult male (pictured)
has red extending from the
cap to the nape. Female has a
red nape, but lacks the red
cap. Young individuals lack
red on the head.

Downy Woodpecker

Dryobates pubescens

L 6" | **WS** 11"

One of the most common and widespread woodpeckers in Ohio, the Downy Woodpecker is best distinguished from the similar Hairy Woodpecker by its smaller size, smaller bill, and black spots on the outer tail. Occurring in nearly any habitat with trees, Downy Woodpeckers regularly visit bird feeders where they especially like suet. Otherwise, they eat a wide variety of insects, fruits, and seeds. Their call is a sharp repeated *pik*, often followed by a trill. During the spring, it is common to hear multiple Downy Woodpeckers' territorial drumming back and forth.

Small with white belly and back, black wings with white barring, and short bill. Males have a red nape on a black-and-white striped head. Female similar but lacks red nape.

Hairy Woodpecker

Dryobates villosus

L 9" | **WS** 14"

Much like the Downy Woodpecker, the Hairy Woodpecker is far more robust, with a proportionately larger bill, and unspotted outer trail feathers. They are fairly common in mature woodlands and well-shaded backyards, parks, and forest edge, and are less likely to be found in smaller woodlots and thin wooded corridors. With this more specific niche, they are not as abundant as "Downies." As with most other woodpeckers, Hairy Woodpeckers frequent bird feeders allowing close inspection. Their typical call is a quick sharp *peek* lower-pitched than Downy. This is often followed by a trill.

Medium-sized, white underparts, black upperparts with white barring, and long bill. Males have a red nape.

Pileated Woodpecker

Dryocopus pileatus

L 17" | **WS** 28"

After a sharp decline in numbers in Ohio from extensive logging in the early 1900s, Pileated Woodpecker populations have recovered statewide and are now uncommon to locally common year-round. More so than other woodpeckers, they prefer larger tracts of mature woodlands, but will occasionally be found in smaller woodlots, corridors and even at backyard bird feeders. Higher concentrations are found in the more forested southern and eastern Ohio, while they are rare and localized in northwestern Ohio, which is dominated by agriculture. The largest and loudest of our resident woodpeckers, they give a series of piping calls, which can be heard from a great distance.

Large crow-size woodpecker mostly black with a large red crest. Face black and white striped. Male (left) with red moustache and forehead; female (below) with black moustache and forehead. In flight, wings two-toned black and white, tail long and black, and neck extended.

Northern Flicker

Colaptes auratus

L 12" **WS** 18"

A multi-colored woodpecker of open forests, parks, woodlots, and backyards, the Northern Flicker is an eye-catcher. Unlike other woodpeckers, Northern Flickers feed largely on ants and often feed on the ground and even on a lawn. Fairly common to common statewide, Northern Flickers are present year-round. In late April to early May, they begin pair-bonding and excavating cavities in dead trees, fence posts, or utility poles. They will also nest in appropriately sized nest boxes. Their call is sometimes described as *flicka flicka flicka* but more realistically it sounds like *wicka wicka wicka*...like a disc jockey.

Boldly patterned, back is brown with black barring, underparts pale with black spotting, black necklace, and head brown and gray with a small red patch on the nape. Male has a black malar stripe, which is lacking on female.

American Kestrel

Falco sparverius

L 10" | **WS** 22"

The American Kestrel is the smallest falcon in North America. These elegant raptors are evenly distributed across the state, preferring open countryside, farmlands, and grasslands, and are present year-round. Sadly, their population has plummeted in recent times, as much as 50 percent, from habitat destruction, predation from larger raptors, and insecticide use. To help their recovery, several organizations came together and created "kestrel highways" by placing nest boxes on the back of road signs along highways, in locations that offer ample hunting grounds. These cavity nesters perch or hover in search of small rodents before ambushing their prey. Their *killy killy killy* call is frequently heard, especially given by territorial birds.

Small falcon. Adult male rusty above with blue-gray wings and black spots. Underparts paler brown with black spots. Face has two black slashes. Female (below) brown overall with darker barring, gray cap, and two black slashes on face.

Merlin
Falco columbarius

L 11" | **WS** 24"

Small and fierce, the Merlin is a petite falcon not much larger than an American Kestrel. In the past they were called Pigeon Hawks due to their pigeon-like flight, but don't let this deceive you—Merlins are powerful and fast. A rare migrant and winter visitor, they are present mostly between September and April. In the summer they are accidental, with singletons reported occasionally. In the past decade a few have nested. Although generally favoring open forests and grasslands Merlins in Ohio have a strong tendency to hang out in urban cemeteries.

Small and stocky. Female and immature brown overall with brown streaking below and a thin eyebrow. Male (below) is gray above and pale below with faint moustache stripe.

Peregrine Falcon

Falco peregrinus

L 17" | **WS** 41"

With a name like Peregrine, meaning wanderer, it's no surprise that Peregrine Falcons are the most widely distributed bird in the world, occurring in a variety of habitats including tundra, deserts, and tropical rainforests. Antarctica is the only continent where they are not found. With the wide use of DDT in the United States, their numbers plummeted landing them on the federal endangered species list. With the banning of these harsh insecticides and the falcons' recent adaptation to urbanization, their numbers have rebounded. Historically they nested almost exclusively on cliffs, but now they can be found nesting on skyscrapers or water towers in many cities, where they prey on birds and bats. Peregrines are best known for their speed. When prey is spotted, they swoop down, fold their wings back, and can reach speeds of up to 240 miles per hour. A feral pigeon won't even see it coming.

In flight, wings long and pointed. Underside of body, wings, and tail heavily barred.

Large falcon with slate-gray back, pale undersides with dark barring. Head has a dark helmet, yellow eye-ring and cere, and sharply hooked bill.

Olive-sided Flycatcher

Contopus cooperi

L 7-8" | **WS** 13"

Olive-sided Flycatchers undertake the longest migration of any North American flycatcher. After departing their wintering grounds as far south as South America, they pass through Ohio around the second through fourth weeks in May, with a few even later into June. After breeding in the Canadian boreal forest, they pass through again in the fall between August and September. Olive-sided Flycatchers tend to be uncommon migrants and always a cause for excitement when found. They are best located perched on top of a tall tree, where they occasionally will swoop down for an insect. The dark gray sides of their breast give them the appearance of wearing a vest. Keep an ear out for their song, which sounds like they are saying *quick-three-beeeers!*

Large elongated flycatcher with a dark "vest" and dark flanks contrasting sharply with pale center. Head tends to look peaked in the rear.

Eastern Wood-Pewee

Contopus virens

L 6" | **WS** 10"

Eastern Wood-Pewees are the most widely distributed flycatcher in Ohio and are usually first detected by their song, a whistled *pee-ah-weee*. A summer breeding resident from South America, pewees start arriving in Ohio by late April, with the majority arriving in May. Occupying virtually any stand of forests or residential areas and parks with large shade trees, Eastern Wood-Pewees perch on branches, swooping down to catch insects before returning back to their perch. By the end of October, all will have departed back south. Eastern Wood-Pewees are distinguished from the *Empidonax* flycatchers by their larger size, longer wings, and darker face. Voice is best for identification.

Medium-sized flycatcher with long wings and tail and peaked crest. Grayish overall with two wing bars.

Yellow-bellied Flycatcher

Empidonax flaviventris

L 5-6" | **WS** 7-8"

Although they may appear drab and nondescript, the Yellow-bellied Flycatcher is the most distinctive *Empidonax* flycatcher in the Eastern U.S. with their strong white eye ring and yellow wash on the belly. A passage migrant only, Yellow-bellied Flycatchers overwinter in Central America and breed in the northern U.S. and Canadian boreal forest and peatlands. In the spring they pass through Ohio from early to mid-May to early June favoring woodlands, forests edge, and thickets. They are generally quiet and easily overlooked. Fall movements are typically more prolonged from late August to early October.

Small yellow-olive flycatcher with two wing bars and a white eye ring. Belly has a variable amount of yellow wash.

Acadian Flycatcher

Empidonax virescens

L 6" | **WS** 9"

Acadian Flycatchers inhabit mature deciduous forests, especially mesic woodlands with streams. They occupy the understories, where they are frequently heard singing *peet-sah* or *pizza* during the spring and summer. Wintering mainly in northwestern South America, Acadian Flycatchers return to Ohio in May and depart by the end of September. Although they have the longest primaries and largest bill of the eastern U.S. *Empidonax* flycatchers, they are still difficult to distinguish from the others, so voice and habitat are keys to identification.

Olive above with wing bars and thin white eye ring. Forehead flat, sloping gently to give a peaked appearance to the head.

Alder Flycatcher & Willow Flycatcher

Empidonax alnorum/traillii

L 6"   **WS** 9"

Alder and Willow Flycatchers are so indistinguishable that they used to be considered one species called "Traill's" Flycatcher. Neotropical migrants, these two flycatchers arrive in Ohio in early to mid-May, with the majority of Alder Flycatchers continuing north into the northern U.S. and Canada. Willow Flycatchers are common breeders statewide in thickets, over-grown pastures, and riparian areas and are quite vocal with their *fitz-bew!* song. Breeding Alder Flycatchers, on the other hand, are restricted to northeastern Ohio where they prefer more wet thickets and damp brushy fields. Their *ree-bee-oh!* song is distinctive. Both species depart from the state by the end of September.

Alder (pictured) and Willow Flycatcher nearly identical. Olive-brown overall with a hint of yellow on the belly. Two white wing bars, white throat, and little to no eye ring.

Least Flycatcher

Empidonax minimus

L 5" | **WS** 8"

The smallest of our *Empidonax* flycatchers in Ohio, the compact Least Flycatcher can be differentiated by its bold white eye ring, large rounded head, and *cheBEK* song, often repeated in a fast sequence. Wintering in Central America, Least Flycatchers are one of the first flycatchers to return to Ohio with some arriving as early as late April. While most continue north, a small number will remain in northern Ohio, especially the northeast, where they will set up territories in second-growth woodlands. Ashtabula County probably holds the largest breeding population in the state. Their fall migration south usually tapers off in early October.

Very small flycatcher with large bold white eye ring and two white wing bars. Grayish-olive above with dusky underparts.

Eastern Phoebe

Sayornis phoebe

L 6" | **WS** 10"

One of the first birds to return in spring, as early as late
February, the Eastern Phoebe is a familiar bird in Ohio.
Breeding statewide usually near water, Eastern Phoebes have
a strong preference for building their nests under bridges and
on buildings along streams, rivers, and ponds. Quite vocal,
their *fee-bee* song, which is often repeated, and their calm
tail-wagging allow for easy identification of this rather plain
species. By early November, most will have returned to their
southern U.S. wintering grounds, but a few remain through
December and even later during mild years.

Grayish-brown above, pale below
with a dark head. Tail constantly
wagging. Lacks distinct wing bars.

Great Crested Flycatcher

Myiarchus crinitus

L 8"   **WS** 13"

The largest flycatcher to occur in Ohio, Great Crested Flycatchers are summer breeding residents between late April and September. They prefer forest openings and edges of deciduous forests, wooded parks, and even neighborhoods with large trees. They are most often detected first by song, a loud whistled *wheep* sometimes followed by an outburst of *prrrt* calls. Our only cavity-nesting flycatcher, Great Crested Flycatchers build nests in old woodpecker holes and will even utilize bird houses specially put up for them. As do other flycatchers, they forage by sitting on a perch swooping down and catching insects.

Big thick-billed flycatcher with large gray peaked head, brown back and wings with rufous primaries, yellow belly extending up to breast, and rufous undertail feathers.

Eastern Kingbird

Tyrannus tyrannus

L 8" | **WS** 14"

This distinctive flycatcher prefers open habitats including overgrown fields, prairies, roadsides, orchards, and woodland edges. A South American wintering species, Eastern Kingbirds are present in Ohio from late April to early September where they are common breeders across the state. Highly territorial and quite aggressive, Eastern Kingbirds defend their nests against other kingbirds and any larger bird that happens to pass by. With their black upperparts, white underparts, and white-tipped tail, they can't be confused with any other species. During displays, their red-orange crown may be visible, but is normally concealed.

Black above becoming darker towards the head, white below. Black square tail is tipped with white.

Northern Shrike

Lanius borealis

L 9" | **WS** 13"

A predatory songbird, Northern Shrikes are winter visitors to Ohio from the north between October and early April. Don't let their size fool you. They are successful predators of small birds and rodents. After catching prey, they will impale it on barbed wire fences or thorn bushes to consume later. They have been known to take prey larger than themselves including Blue Jays and Mourning Doves. Occurring in semi-open habitats such as overgrown fields and meadows, they typically sit on top of a bush or small tree watching their surroundings. Areas that tend to host this species annually include Magee Marsh, Mosquito Creek, Killdeer Plains and Delaware Wildlife Areas, as well as the reclaimed strip mine areas around The Wilds. If you stumble upon a shrike during the summer, you may have found a Loggerhead Shrike, which is now extirpated from Ohio but shows up occasionally.

Chunky gray bird with black mask, wings, and tail. Black bill hooked. In flight has white wing patches.

White-eyed Vireo

Vireo griseus

L 5" | **WS** 7"

The White-eyed Vireo is normally detected first by its persistent singing, often said to be saying *pick up the beer CHECK!* A common to uncommon bird of thickets and brushy habitats, they are most abundant in the southern and eastern regions of Ohio, becoming more localized in the northwest. Present from mid-April to mid-October, White-eyed Vireos are best distinguished by their two wing bars and white eyes surrounded by yellow spectacles.

Small and gray-headed with yellow lores extending around the white eyes. Olive-green back with two wing bars. Bill thick with slight hook at the tip.

Bell's Vireo
Vireo bellii

L 5" | **WS** 7"

A bird of brushy thickets and overgrown fields, the Bell's Vireo breeds throughout the Southwest and Midwest, and over the past few decades has slowly expanded into western and central Ohio. A rare summer resident and breeder, Bell's Vireos arrive from their Mexican wintering grounds in May and depart Ohio by mid-September. An active songster, they are typically heard singing their *cheedle cheedle cheedle chew!* song from an exposed branch; otherwise they remain concealed in thick shrubs. Glacier Ridge and Battelle Darby Creek Metro Parks in Columbus have been very reliable in recent years among other parks between Cincinnati and Columbus.

Small and warbler-like but larger thick bill with slight hook at tip. Brownish-gray with two wing bars, the top one less distinct. Flanks typically have a wash of yellow.

Yellow-throated Vireo
Vireo flavifrons

L 6" | **WS** 9"

The Yellow-throated Vireo is a common to uncommon denizen of open deciduous forests, where it favors a well-developed canopy. More often heard than seen, their song is like the more common Red-eyed Vireo but lower pitched with a burry quality. Wintering in Central and South America and the Caribbean, these Neotropical migrants are present in Ohio from mid-April to early October. They favor the more wooded regions of southern and eastern Ohio, though they can be found statewide. More colorful than our other vireos, the Yellow-throated Vireo has a yellow-green head, yellow throat, bright yellow spectacles, and white wing bars.

Stocky with olive-green head, yellow spectacles and breast, and white belly. Two distinctive white wing bars. Bill thick and hooked at the tip.

Blue-headed Vireo

Vireo solitarius

L 6" | **WS** 9"

The Blue-headed Vireo is a common migrant through Ohio in the spring (Apr-May) and fall (Sep-Oct) occupying any wooded habitat. Breeding is restricted to northeastern Ohio where they are the only species of vireo that regularly breeds in coniferous forests. Mohican Forest, Cuyahoga Valley National Park, and the hemlock gorges along the Lake and Geauga County border play host to a good number of breeding pairs. Their song is a sweeter and slower version of Red-eyed Vireo with a slurred quality. With their blue-gray head and obvious white spectacles, no other species in Ohio looks anything like these.

Small stocky bird with blue-gray head, thick bill, white spectacles and lores, white belly with yellowish flanks, and olive-green back with two white wing bars.

Philadelphia Vireo

Vireo philadelphicus

L 5" | **WS** 9"

Philadelphia Vireos are easily overlooked and frequently passed off as a Warbling Vireo, which is far more common in Ohio. Closer inspection, however, will reveal a distinctive yellow wash to their throat and underparts. An uncommon migrant, the majority pass through the state in May on their way north into Canada where they are the most northern breeding vireo. Fall migration is generally from late August through October. Their song is reminiscent of Red-eyed Vireo, but higher and slower *Here I am, See me– Up here*. Contrary to their name, they are not a common migrant through Philadelphia, but the first specimen was collected there.

Small and stocky. Overall rather plain except for yellow on the throat and belly. Grayish cap with a paler supercilium. Thick bill hooked at the tip.

Warbling Vireo
Vireo gilvus

L 5" | **WS** 9"

Favoring large trees near water, Warbling Vireos are common in riparian areas and along lakes and reservoirs, especially where willows and cottonwoods are present. Although rather visually plain, the Warbling Vireo has a joyful warbling song and is quite vocal during the spring and summer. A Neotropical migrant from Central America, Warbling Vireos are present in Ohio from mid-April to early October throughout the state. This is by far one of the most commonly heard summer residents in the western Lake Erie basin, which has some of the best habitat for them in the state.

Very plain and nondescript vireo. Small and stocky, upperparts grayish and underparts pale. Pale supercilium and no wing bars. Thick bill with hooked tip.

Red-eyed Vireo

Vireo olivaceus

L 5" | **WS** 10"

One of the most common breeding birds in deciduous forests throughout Ohio and the eastern U.S., Red-eyed Vireos are Neotropical migrants from South America that are present in the state from April to October. Breeding occurs in mature forests as well as in wooded residential neighborhoods, parks, and large wooded lots. Their song suggests that they are lost *here I am, where are you– I'm over here!* but they are clearly not lost, as nearly a million are estimated to breed in Ohio annually. Quite the songsters, they will sing all day long even during the mid-day heat, so they are easy to locate...but to see one takes a little more effort because they prefer the thick foliage of the canopy.

Olive-green vireo with gray cap, pale supercilium, red eyes, and pale underparts. Large thick bill hooked at the tip.

Blue Jay

Cyanocitta cristata

L 11" | **WS** 15"

Ubiquitous and lively, the Blue Jay is a very familiar species across Ohio to birders and non-birders alike. Abundant in any forested habitat including residential neighborhoods, city parks, cemeteries, and backyard bird feeders, Blue Jays feed on a variety of food items including nuts, seeds, berries, and even baby birds and eggs. Related to crows, Blue Jays are in the corvid family and are present all year long. During the spring, impressive numbers can be seen migrating along the Lake Erie coast, especially east of Toledo, where tens of thousands are possible. This is because Lake Erie acts as a natural barrier that they don't like crossing. Instead, they find a way around the lake. Boisterous and loud, Blue Jays have a wide repertoire of calls and are great mimics of Red-shouldered Hawk.

Large with blue upperparts and white underparts. Wings and tail have black barring. Large crest and black necklace obvious. Small white wing bar. In flight, outer tail feathers white.

American Crow

Corvus brachyrhynchos

L 18" | **WS** 37"

The American Crow is an abundant year-round resident throughout the state, occurring in habitats ranging from open farmlands to forested areas and urban centers. Ubiquitous and clever, their numbers have increased in Ohio with the clearing of forests, but they are also a particular victim to West Nile Virus. Crows roost communally outside the breeding season, especially near cities, where thousands can be found in a single roost. In recent years, a small population of the similar Fish Crow has taken up residence around Cleveland, particularly near Shaker Heights. They are best differentiated by voice with the American Crow giving a typical *caw-caw-caw,* while the Fish Crow has a softer *nah-uh.*

Large and entirely black. Can appear glossy in certain lighting.

Horned Lark
Eremophila alpestris

L 7" | **WS** 13"

Horned Larks prefer farmlands, hayfields and pasture, and
have adapted well to Ohio's changing landscape as forests were
cleared for agriculture. In the spring and summer their musical
tinkling songs are commonly heard over fields, and they are
most abundant in northern and western Ohio. During the
winter, flocks of Horned Larks can be found in corn stubble and
other farmland often mixed with other birds including Lapland
Longspurs. Known as a "Shorelark" in the Old World, Horned
Larks are also found in Europe, Asia, and Africa.

Sparrow-like, brownish above and paler below with a thin black breast band. Adult male has little ear tufts, hence the name Horned Lark. Their black mask is bordered by yellow above and below. Female is less distinctive and lacks the black mask.

Northern Rough-winged Swallow

Stelgidopteryx serripennis

L 6" | **WS** 11"

Brown above, and pale below, the Northern Rough-winged Swallow is a nondescript swallow of riparian areas. Favoring streams where they nest in exposed riverbanks, these common swallows will also take up residency in a variety of other available sites including drain pipes under bridges and gutters. They are present in Ohio from late March through October and feed on insects while airborne, often giving their low *bzzt bzzt* calls. The name "rough-winged" refers to tiny hooks on their primary feathers. To the touch, these hooks are rough.

In flight, wings long and pointed and tail squared.

Elongated body, all brown above with white belly and dusky breast and throat.

Purple Martin
Progne subis

L 8" **WS** 16"

Purple Martins are large dark swallows that occur throughout Ohio from late March through September. Closely associated to humans, Purple Martins historically nested in tree cavities but now nest almost exclusively in "condos"–houses or gourds provided by humans. Preferably these nesting colonies are placed near humans and a water source. This change in breeding habits extends back to the Native Americans, who would hang hollowed-out gourds above their crops–perhaps to chase off crows or to manage insects. Now large colonies can be found around parks, reservoirs, and especially within Amish communities. Their liquid gurgling calls are pleasing to the ears.

Large and stocky. Adult male iridescent dark blue to purple with dark wings and forked tail.

Female and immature duller with a gray face, chest, and collar.

Tree Swallow

Tachycineta bicolor

L 6" | **WS** 13"

One of the most common swallows in Ohio, the Tree Swallow is also the hardiest; some birds return as early as late February. An abundant breeder throughout the state, Tree Swallows nest in dead trees and bird boxes, typically near water sources such as lakes, reservoirs, ponds, and wetlands. Any wetland with standing dead trees with plenty of woodpecker holes will almost certainly have nesting Tree Swallows. Their vocalizations are melodic with various twittering and high-pitched calls. In the late fall, large concentrations in the hundreds or even thousands form before migrating south and are quite the spectacle. Most will depart the state by mid-November.

Male is iridescent blue, sometimes blue-green above and white below with a small black mask.

Female is like male, but mostly brown above with only a little hint of blue. Younger birds are entirely brown above.

Bank Swallow

Riparia riparia

L 5" | **WS** 11"

The small Bank Swallow is a Neotropical migrant, which arrives in Ohio in April and usually departs by the end of September. Like Northern Rough-winged Swallows, the Bank Swallow utilizes steep banks adjacent to streams, rivers, and quarries for nesting, but typically occurs in large colonies. They excavate their burrows near the top of the bank using their bill, feet, and wings sometimes up to a few feet deep. In Ohio they occur statewide and are most common along the northern tier near Lake Erie. With their dark breast band, they are not likely to be confused with other swallows.

rown upperparts and pale
nderparts with a dark breast band.
flight (inset), small with white belly,
rown wings, and dark breast band.

Barn Swallow

Hirundo rustica

L 7" | **WS** 12"

The Barn Swallow is a common summer resident of open countryside. Present from late March through October, Barn Swallows breed statewide under the eaves of barns, sheds, and under bridges, where they build a nest made of mud. They consume a large number of insects, which is beneficial to humans. Watch for these deeply fork-tailed swallows over farm fields and grasslands as they feed. They are usually vocal as they feed, giving a rapid mechanical twittering.

In flight has the longest forked tail of any swallow. Very tawny below with distinctive rusty throat.

Sleek with steel-blue upperparts, tawny underparts, and rusty forehead and throat. Wings and tail long and pointed

Cliff Swallow

Petrochelidon pyrrhonota

L 5" | **WS** 12"

Prior to the 1820s, Cliff Swallows did not occur in Ohio or much of the eastern U.S. With the clearing of forests, they moved in and by the late 1800s their numbers peaked. Since then, their numbers have declined considerably. Nonetheless, they remain locally common in large breeding colonies under bridges and on dam walls of reservoirs, where they build nests out of mud. This is a change from their original breeding locations as suggested by their name. Present from April to September, they are common at most inland reservoirs and along Lake Erie. Some will breed under the eaves of barns and other buildings such as the Maumee Bay State Park lodge. Colonies are typically vocal with a soft *chur* given by many individuals as they fly around.

Dark and compact with a dark blue back, cinnamon rump, and pale underparts. The face is chestnut with a blue cap and pale forehead. In flight, the tail is squared off at the end.

Black-capped Chickadee

Poecile atricapilla

L 5-6" | **WS** 6-8"

The common and confiding chickadee of northern Ohio, Black-capped Chickadees occur from Lima, Mansfield, Canton, and Steubenville north. Abundant in virtually any habitat with trees from woodlands to parks and suburban neighborhoods. A permanent resident, these active birds are constantly on the move gleaning trees for insects and visiting backyard bird feeders. They are best distinguished from their southern counterpart, the Carolina Chickadee, by their voice and range, though their range largely overlaps and hybrids are possible. The Black-capped song is a whistled *fee bee* and their call is a raspy *chick-a-dee-dee-dee*. Visually, they are differentiated from Carolina by their somewhat ragged black bib, not clean-cut.

Small and active. Black cap and bib contrasts with white cheeks. Gray wings have white edging. Underparts buffy.

Carolina Chickadee

Poecile atricapilla

L 4-5" | **WS** 6-8"

More widespread in Ohio than the similar Black-capped Chickadee, the Carolina Chickadee occurs in all but the far northern part of state typically south of US-224. Hybrids can be expected where their ranges overlap. These confiding, energetic birds occur in any forested habitat including woodlands, parks, neighborhoods, and backyard bird feeders. Carolina has a longer song than their northern counterpart, a whistled *fee-bee fee-bay* and also gives a *chick-a-dee-dee-dee* call but much quicker. Their black bibs also tend to be much cleaner and sharply defined than Black-capped. With patience, chickadees can be enticed to taking seeds from one's hand.

Small, long-tailed, and energetic with a black cap and big, white cheeks, and gray back and wings.

Tufted Titmouse

Baeolophus bicolor

L 6" | **WS** 9"

The Tufted Titmouse is a common permanent resident statewide occurring in woodlands, parks, and suburban neighborhoods. Recognized for their gray plumage, crested head, black forehead, and rusty flanks, they are not like any other species. Much like chickadees, the Tufted Titmouse is a regular backyard inhabitant that frequents bird feeders. They typically announce their presence with their *peter-peter-peter* song and various contact calls and hissing. A cavity nester, the Tufted Titmouse will use woodpecker cavities and bird houses. The Tufted Titmouse has expanded its range northward during the past century, a movement often associated with an increase in winter bird feeders and possibly a warming climate.

Small and gray with a crest, black forehead, long tail, and rusty flanks.

Red-breasted Nuthatch

Sitta canadensis

L 5" | **WS** 8"

The Red-breasted Nuthatch is a resident of northern boreal forests and montane coniferous forests. In Ohio they are mainly a migrant and winter visitor between August and May. Numbers vary year to year with irregular irruptions when there is a food shortage up north. In some winters they are present in small numbers, while in others they can be very common occurring in nearly every patch of pine or spruce. A rare summer resident, a few nest mainly in the northeastern corner of the state, especially around Cuyahoga Valley National Park. Often, they are first detected by their hornlike *ank-ank-ank* emitted from a coniferous tree. Like other nuthatches, they forage upwards, downwards, and sideways along tree trunks. A regular visitor to bird feeders, they especially enjoy suet.

Small and compact, gray above, rusty below, with a black-and-white striped head. Often foraging head-first down a tree.

White-breasted Nuthatch
Sitta carolinensis

L 5" | **WS** 10"

This "upside-down" bird is best identified by its habit of
foraging head-first down tree trunks. A very common and widespread resident throughout Ohio, White-breasted Nuthatches
prefer forested habitats including wooded suburban backyards
and bird feeders. Their common name refers to their knack of
jamming acorns or nuts into bark and pecking them to "hatch"
out the seed. In winter, nuthatches, chickadees, and titmice
will come together to forage, which helps them to find food and
watch for predators. Their song is a quick *hah-hah-hah-hah* and
their call is a nasal *yank-yank-yank*.

Compact and no neck.
Gray above, white below
with a black cap, and a
rusty wash near the rear.

Brown Creeper

Certhia americana

L 5" | **WS** 7"

The mottled brown back of the Brown Creeper keeps it well-camouflaged when creeping up tree trunks. Unlike nuthatches, which typically move downward headfirst, Brown Creepers fly to the base of a tree and creep upward. Often difficult to see, they are best located by their high-pitched *seee* call and in spring, their series of high-pitched notes lasting a couple of seconds. Present in Ohio year-round, they are most commonly seen in spring and fall migration and in winter when they occur in any wooded habitat, especially mature woodland. The breeding range of the Brown Creeper in Ohio is mostly restricted to the northeast, but over the last few decades, they have expanded southwest toward Dayton. Nest placement is typically behind peeling bark of dead trees and some living trees such as Shagbark Hickories. No other bird is likely confused with the Brown Creeper.

Small, slim, and incredibly cryptic. Upperparts mottled brown, underparts white, bill thin and decurved, and tail spine-tipped.

House Wren

Troglodytes aedon

L 5" | **WS** 7"

The tiny musical House Wren is a common summer resident from April through September statewide, favoring gardens, thickets, shrubs, woodland edges, and suburbia. Our plainest wren, this restless species builds a stick nest in cavities and has a strong preference for human-made bird boxes. Aggressive and territorial, they are well known for evicting Eastern Bluebirds and Tree Swallows and taking over their nest boxes. House Wrens are known to add spider egg sacs to their nest. When the spiders hatch, they help control mite and other parasite infestations. This wren's loud bubbly song is commonly heard and when a wren is alarmed, it gives harsh scolding calls.

Small and compact. Brown with a short tail, short decurved bill, pale throat, and dark baring on wings and tail.

Winter Wren

Troglodytes hiemalis

L 4" | **WS** 6"

The diminutive Winter Wren, weighing only a half an ounce, makes up for its size by its incredible song. Using two voice boxes, these songsters sing a continuous musical song for eight or more seconds with their head tilted back, tail shaking, and chest pushed out. Winter Wrens are an uncommon migrant and winter visitor from late September through May when they prefer the understory of mature forests. In the summer, they are localized to a few sites in northeast Ohio where they breed in hemlock gorges most notably at the Holden Arboretum, Mohican State Forest, and Cuyahoga Valley National Park.

Small and round. Brown and barred overall, short stubby tail usually held upward, and faint pale supercilium. Darker than similar House Wren, which lacks the supercilium.

Sedge Wren
Cistothorus platensis

L 4" | **WS** 7"

A small denizen of sedge meadows, grassy margins of wetlands, and drier habit such as hayfields and upland pastures, Sedge Wrens are the scarcest wrens that occur in Ohio. They are present from April through September and tend to be erratic at their breeding sites. In some years they are present and in other years they are absent, and their arrival time in the spring and early summer has no obvious pattern. Avoiding the unglaciated region, which lacks their preferred habitat, most Sedge Wrens are found in northern, central, and southwestern Ohio. They are most often detected first by their song consisting of 3-4 sharp chips followed by a trill. Battelle Darby Creek Metro Park, Killdeer Plains and Pickerel Creek Wildlife Areas, and Ottawa National Wildlife Refuge are fairly reliable areas to find this scarce breeder.

Small wren with streaked back and cap, banded wings, and plain peachy underparts. Tail often held upward.

Marsh Wren

Cistothorus palustris

L 5″ | **WS** 7″

A boisterous denizen of cattail marshes, the Marsh Wren lurks deep in vegetation occasionally teeing up on a cattail to sing. A summer resident and breeder, most arrive in April and depart by the end of October. Occurring throughout the state, Marsh Wrens are most abundant in the western Lake Erie basin at places such as Magee Marsh Wildlife Area, Ottawa National Wildlife Refuge and Mallard Club Marsh, and they decrease in numbers in the southeast where there is less favorable habitat. A small number overwinter annually especially at Battelle Darby Creek Metro Park and Killbuck Marsh Wildlife Area. They are typically first detected by a series of musical bubbly gurgles followed by a trill.

Tiny round wren with a short tail often held upward. Upperparts rusty-brown with black and white streaks down the back while the underparts are paler lacking streaking. Note the white supercilium.

Carolina Wren

Thryothorus ludovicianus

L 5" | **WS** 8"

A familiar bird of backyards, gardens, and suburbia as well as rural areas, the Carolina Wren favors dense undergrowth and scrub. They are common and widespread throughout Ohio becoming more abundant farther south. Historically Carolina Wrens were a southern species and did not occur in northern Ohio. With the warming climate, they have expanded north into the Great Lakes and into southern Canada. With periodical cold snaps during the winter, these northern populations will occasionally take a hit, but tend to rebound quickly. Often nesting in close quarters to humans, the Carolina Wren's *tea-kettle tea-kettle tea-kettle* song is a welcome sound.

Our largest wren. Bright rusty-brown above and warm buffy below with a long white eyebrow, white throat, and long tail often held upward.

Blue-gray Gnatcatcher

Polioptila caerulea

L 4" | **WS** 6"

The tiny Blue-gray Gnatcatcher is a common migrant and summer breeding resident across Ohio, arriving in April. Preferring deciduous woodlands and neighboring scrub, they are often found in parks and backyards. Easily detected by call, Blue-gray Gnatcatchers give a fussy high-pitched call while they forage in the tree canopy. Their long tail frequently flicks back and forth, which helps to scare up their insect food. Their nests are well constructed with spider webs and lichen and often look like a knot in the tree. Most depart south by the end of October.

Blue-gray above, white below with a black tail and white outer tail feathers. White eye ring conspicuous, while breeding males have a distinctive black eyebrow often giving them a fierce look.

Golden-crowned Kinglet

Regulus satrapa

L 4" | **WS** 6"

Among the smallest birds in Ohio, Golden-crowned Kinglets
are a resilient species overwintering in Ohio despite frigid
temperatures, where they find wintering caterpillars. They
are most common in the state during spring and fall migration
particularly in April and October but can be found throughout
the winter where they favor woodlands, especially coniferous
trees. Northbound migrants linger in Ohio as late as mid-May.
Like the Ruby-crowned Kinglet, the Golden-crowned actively
moves around in constant motion often wing-flicking, however
their crown is a brilliant orange-yellow setting these two
diminutive species apart. Interestingly, DNA suggests the
Golden-crowned Kinglet is more closely related to the Gold-
crest, its European counterpart, than it is to the Ruby-crowned
back at home. Listen for their thin, quiet *tsee tsee tsee* often
heard from the tree canopy.

Small with tiny bill,
faintly marked black and
white face stripes, and
yellow to orange crown
with black bordering.

Ruby-crowned Kinglet

Regulus calendula

L 4″ | **WS** 7″

A tiny songbird with a proportionally large head, Ruby-crowned Kinglets energetically forage among trees for food, actively flicking their wings and often hovering in flight to investigate a leaf. They are abundant migrants in the spring (Apr-May) and fall (Sep-Nov) virtually anywhere with trees, often mixed with warblers and other migrants. While Golden-crowned Kinglets regularly overwinter, Ruby-crowned tends to winter farther south in the U.S., though a few hardier individuals will stick around. The majority of these will eventually head south or perish in the colder temperatures come January and February. They are often detected first by their fast, two-noted *ji-dit* call. In spring they give a series of soft high notes followed by a musical spiral of notes, often perceived as a larger bird.

Small olive-green bird with tiny bill and tail. White eye ring and single wing bar obvious. Male individuals occasionally display their red crown, often when excited.

Eastern Bluebird

Sialia sialis

L 7" | **WS** 12"

One of the most beloved birds in Ohio, the Eastern Bluebird used to be abundant across the state, preferring old fields, orchards, roadsides, and parks. With the change in agriculture to more monoculture and the increase in the non-native House Sparrow, which competes with the bluebirds for nesting, their numbers have declined as much as 90 percent. However, with homemade bird boxes and dedicated bluebird trail volunteers, Eastern Bluebirds have made a comeback. Present year-round throughout the state, Eastern Bluebirds are easily recognized by their stunning blue backs and orange breasts and are regularly seen perched on powerlines and fencerows.

Male bright blue above, orange neck, breast, and flanks, and white belly. Regularly nests in bird houses.

Juvenile brown and spotted overall with blue in the wings and tail. Often has a wide-eyed appearance.

Female like male but much fainter overall in coloration.

American Robin

Turdus migratorius

L 10" | **WS** 14"

The American Robin hardly needs an introduction as one of the most common and widespread birds in North America. Common on lawns, golf courses, parks, gardens, and in wooded areas, robins are well established across Ohio. Often reported as the earliest species to return in spring, American Robins are actually year-round residents in Ohio. Only some of our birds migrate south for the winter. In the summer they feed on insects and earthworms and in winter they form loose flocks and feed on berries. Breeding takes place from April through July when they lay blue eggs in nests often built near houses including porches, sheds, and other structures. Spring and summers in Ohio wouldn't be the same without the cheerful dawn chorus of robins singing their whistled *cheery up, cheery up, cheerily, cherry, cheery up* song. Their alarm call is a sharp *peek*.

Adult male gray on back and wings, rusty belly, dark head with white spectacles, yellow bill, and black and white streaked throat.

Juvenile heavily spotted on back and chest.

Adult female similar to male but much duller overall.

Veery
Catharus fuscescens

L 7" | **WS** 11"

An inhabitant of damp deciduous woodlands and disturbed and second-growth habitats, the Veery is a common spring migrant in Ohio during May. Breeding, however, is restricted primarily to the northeastern corner of the state in places such as Mohican State Forest and Cuyahoga Valley National Park. The forests of Hocking County in the southeast also host a decent number. Sadly, their numbers have decreased rapidly during the last few decades, and they are becoming a scarce breeder in Ohio. Where they persist, their harmonious descending song is simply breathtaking. By the end of July most breeding residents are quiet, and they are not often detected until late August through September during their southbound fall migration. Their namesake comes from their contact call, an abrupt *VEER*.

Medium-sized plump thrush, rich cinnamon-brown above. Underparts pale with light spotting on breast.

Gray-cheeked Thrush

Catharus minimus

L 6-7"   **WS** 13"

The Gray-cheeked Thrush is a migrant through Ohio during spring (May) and fall (Aug-Sep) migration. They tend to be less common and more secretive than our other thrushes and are best found by examining the more common Swainson's Thrushes for individuals with gray instead of buffy faces. From their wintering grounds in South America, Gray-cheeked Thrushes undergo an impressive migration heading farther north than other thrushes to breed in taiga and Arctic shrub thickets in Canada, Alaska, and even eastern Siberia. In 2015 the research team at Black Swamp Bird Observatory caught an individual at their banding station east of Magee Marsh, which was banded in Colombia in the previous year.

Uniform brown overall with paler underparts. Broad eye ring and grayish face lacking any buffy color, separate it from the similar Swainson's Thrush.

Swainson's Thrush

Catharus ustulatus

L 7" | **WS** 12"

A common spring and fall migrant, the Swainson's Thrush can be found throughout the state from late April through May and August to November, where they occupy dense undergrowth, deciduous forest, swamp forests, and parks. A nocturnal migrant, their call note overhead resembles a Spring Peeper, a hollow *peep*. Swainson's Thrushes typically forage low, feeding on bugs and berries either by hopping along the ground or foraging on low branches and logs. Similar to the Gray-cheeked Thrush, Swainson's are more abundant and have a noticeably buffy face and eye ring, setting these two species apart.

Olive-brown above and white below with dark brown spotting on throat and breast. Face and spectacles buffy, unlike other species of thrush.

Hermit Thrush

Catharus guttatus

L 7" | **WS** 11"

A thrush typically associated with northern forests, the Hermit Thrush breeds in a few patches of suitable habitat and hemlock forests in northeastern Ohio including Mohican State Forest and Cuyahoga Valley National Park as well as Hocking Hills State Park, Conkles Hollow State Nature Reserve, and Clear Creek Metro Park in southeastern Ohio. In these areas, their haunting ethereal song echoes through the understory. Outside of breeding season, Hermit Thrushes are more common statewide during spring and fall migration, mainly in April and from September to early November. A hardy species, some remain in Ohio throughout the winter, becoming more regular to the south. During migration and summer, Hermit Thrushes feed on insects and switch to fruits, particularly berries, during the winter. Their habit of flicking their wings and slowly raising and lowering their tail, in addition to their rusty reddish tail, set this species apart from the other thrushes.

smaller, full-bodied thrush ith brown upperparts, white nderparts, and dark spotting n throat and breast. Their eddish tail is diagnostic, often aised and lowered slowly.

Wood Thrush

Hylocichla mustelina

L 8" | **WS** 13"

The flute-like descending song of the Wood Thrush fills Ohio's deciduous woodlands in the spring and summer. These ethereal notes are created by the divided syrinx (vocal tube), which allows two separate notes to produce song simultaneously. Wood Thrushes can inhabit extensive woodlands to several-acre woodlots as long as closed canopy is present. Arriving in mid-April, the Wood Thrush is common throughout the state through July and is less detected from August to departure in October. They become more silent during the height of breeding season. Sadly, the destruction and fragmentation of forests in Ohio and in their wintering grounds in Mexico and Central America have resulted in a sharp decline in Wood Thrush numbers, but today they still remain common throughout the state.

Larger pot-bellied thrush with an upright posture. Reddish above and white below with extensive black spotting on the breast, more than on other thrushes.

Gray Catbird

Dumetella carolinensis

L 9" | **WS** 11"

The Gray Catbird is a fairly common resident statewide from April through October. The genus name *Dumetella* means "small thicket," which describes their preferred habitat of leafy thickets, overgrown brushy fields, hedges, and gardens. Although they are part of the mimid family, they are not as versatile as mockingbirds at mimicking other bird songs. However, they do have a complex repertoire of single-sylla-bled whistles, squeaks, and chatters, and especially a cat-like *meew*—hence their common name. The vast majority of these migrants overwinter in the southeastern and Gulf Coast states, though a few hardy individuals may be found throughout the winter in Ohio especially during mild winters.

niform gray overall
ith a black cap
nd rufous undertail
overts. Medium-
zed with short
ings and long tail.

Brown Thrasher

Toxostoma rufum

L 11" | **WS** 12"

A bird of forest edge, dense shrub, and second-growth habitats, the Brown Thrasher is often first detected by song. Their large repertoire, with notes always repeated in pairs, is unlike the Northern Mockingbird, which repeats each note three or more times. When not singing from a high prominent perch, these reddish-brown mimids are typically found on the ground where they thrash around in leaf litter in search of insects, seeds, and berries. They are expected throughout Ohio from mid-March through mid-October but are occasionally detected during the winter.

A fairly large songbird with long tail and slightly curved bill. Reddish-brown above and pale below with bold dark streaks.

Northern Mockingbird

Mimus polyglottos

L 9" | **WS** 13"

Contrary to the name, Northern Mockingbirds tend to be a
southern species and probably arrived in Ohio only in the
twentieth century. As their name implies, mockingbirds have a
remarkable repertoire of up to 200 different song types, mostly
"mocking" (that is, mimicking) the calls and songs of other
local birds. These mimicked songs sometimes lead birders
to misidentify them as other species based only on the song.
They will sing throughout the day and even during the night.
Northern Mockingbirds are most at home in mixed habitat of
open country with scattered trees and especially fruit-bearing
shrubs and often quite common in overgrown industrial areas.
Fierce and territorial, mockingbirds are frequently seen
chasing other birds from their territory. Occurring throughout
Ohio, they are most common to the south and east. Some areas
in northern Ohio lack them altogether.

Medium-sized and slender
with long tail. Gray above and
paler below with two
prominent wing bars. In flight,
white wing patches and white
outer tail feathers diagnostic.

European Starling

Sturnus vulgaris

L 8" | **WS** 14"

One of the most ubiquitous species in Ohio, European Starlings are found in practically every corner of the state in nearly all habitat types, excluding deep mature woodland. In the 1890s these starlings were introduced into New York City and by 1916, they had reached Ohio. By the mid-1920s, they became established across Ohio. Sadly, as with many other non-native species, the European Starling has had a negative impact on some of our native birds, most notably woodpeckers. Among their preferred nesting sites are woodpecker holes, and they aggressively evict woodpeckers from their nesting cavities. Quite the songsters, European Starlings give whistles and jumbled warbling, sometimes including mimicry of other bird species.

Chunky and short-tailed. Breeding adult dark with purplish-green iridescence and bright yellow bill.

Juvenile brown overall with dark bill.

In winter, heavily spotted on back and underparts. Bill darker than breeding adults, typically turning yellow by spring.

Cedar Waxwing

Bombycilla cedrorum

L 6" | **WS** 11"

The elegant Cedar Waxwing is one of Ohio's most striking birds.
Occurring in a wide variety of habitats including woodlands,
parks, cemeteries, suburban neighborhoods, and riparian corridors, Cedar Waxwings have a strong fondness for berries. Whether
native berries such as dogwood and serviceberry or non-native
ornamentals, waxwings travel around in nomadic flocks in
search of fruiting trees. Breeding typically begins in June when
they switch to more of an insect diet. Often Cedar Waxwings
will start a second brood in late summer, but many of these are
failed attempts. During any time of year, keep an ear out for their
soft whistled *tseee-tseeee* calls, which can push the limits of
our hearing ability. During the winter watch for the Bohemian
Waxwing, which is a scarce visitor to Ohio and occasionally turns
up in Cedar Waxwing flocks. Their larger size and rusty undertail
coverts distinguish them from Cedar Waxwings.

Juvenile like adult but
heavily streaked. Black
mask less prominent.

Adult striking with prominent crest, contrasting dark mask on brown head, and yellow belly. Back and wings change from brown to gray downward, and there is distinctive yellow tip on the tail. Red tips on the secondaries visible on some individuals.

American Goldfinch

Spinus tristis

L 5" | **WS** 8"

The striking male American Goldfinch is hard to miss in the summer with its bright yellow plumage. Often mistakenly called a "yellow canary," American Goldfinches are year-round residents throughout the state where they occur in weedy fields, parks, gardens, bird feeders, and overgrown areas. Their vegetarian diet consists almost entirely of seeds, especially thistle, and they often perch atop a stem to pluck the seeds. Because of their diet of late-seeding plants, they are one of our latest breeders in the state, often nesting in late July and early August when thistle and other fibrous plants are producing seeds. Their characteristic *po-ta-to-chip, po-ta-to-chip* call is often heard as they fly over in undulating flight. Males will also give a *tee-yee* call note, which is often followed by their musical song.

In summer, breeding male bright yellow with black forehead and black wings with white markings.

During winter, nonbreeding and immature birds tan with a yellowish tinge. Males have black wings, and females have dusky wings. Bill dark.

Breeding female dull yellow with dusky wings with white markings.

Common Redpoll

Acanthis flammea

L 5" | **WS** 8"

The Common Redpoll is an irregular winter visitor to Ohio between October and April. In most years very few show up south of the Great Lakes, but following seed crop failures farther north, large numbers may irrupt south and often congregate at bird feeders and on birch trees. Listen for flocks overhead, which are evident by their buzzy calls and lively trills. Highly nomadic, an individual banded in Michigan was found again in Siberia, while others banded in Alaska have turned up in the eastern U.S.

Small finch with tiny pointed bill. Upperparts and flanks heavily streaked. Adult male has red crown and rosy-washed chest. Female (inset) like male but lacks red coloration.

Pine Siskin

Spinus pinus

L 5" | **WS** 8"

The gregarious Pine Siskin is an uncommon to common winter visitor depending on the status of the seed crop farther north. Highly nomadic, when seed crops fail, large numbers irrupt south with some flocks numbering in the hundreds. These flocks are always chatty with wheezy contact calls, harsh upsweeping *zrreeeeet* calls, and *tit-a, tit-a-tit* flight calls, and often invade bird feeders filled with nyjer seed. After large flight years, some opportunistic Pine Siskins will remain in Ohio during the summer to breed. Breeding typically takes place in ornamental conifers in residential yards, parks, and cemeteries.

Small finch with pointed bill. Brown and streaky overall with yellow on the wings and tail.

House Finch

Haemorhous mexicanus

L 6" | **WS** 9"

The House Finch, originally occurring only west of the Mississippi River, was accidentally introduced in New York City in 1940. The first one reached Ohio (Lake County) in 1964 and by the 1970s, they were well established throughout the state. Today House Finches are most common in residential yards from cities to rural farmland, especially if dense shrubbery is present. Many will nest in hanging flower pots and under awnings of houses, hence their name. Throughout the spring and summer, their jumbled warbling song is a frequent attraction in our backyards. They are common year-round, compared to the Purple Finch, which is mostly present in the state during the winter. Both species regularly visit bird feeders.

Small finch with rosy-red face and breast, brown streaking on back and belly, and a notched tail. Female (inset) like male but lacking red on face and breast. Lacks supercilium seen on the female Purple Finch.

Purple Finch

Haemorhous purpureus

L 6" | **WS** 10"

The Purple Finch is a year-round resident throughout Ohio where it prefers coniferous forests, ornamental conifers in residential properties, and other wooded areas. They are most often seen during spring (Apr-May) and fall (Sep-Nov) migration when small groups can show up just about anywhere, often at bird feeders. Winter numbers fluctuate from year to year depending on food sources farther north and weather. In summer, Purple Finches are restricted to the northeastern corner of the state, where they are an uncommon breeding resident in places such as Mohican State Forest, Cuyahoga Valley National Park, and the Holden Arboretum. Male Purple Finches give a rich warbling song ending in a high emphatic note. Females will also sing, as will immature males which look like females. Both sexes give a finch-like *tek* call.

Small finch. Male raspberry red head, breast and back; conical seed-eating bill. Female (inset) and immature heavily streaked above and below.

Evening Grosbeak
Coccothraustes vespertinus

L 7" | **WS** 13"

The Evening Grosbeak has a colossal bill. Its scientific name *Coccothraustes* means "kernel crusher," which appropriately suits this striking yellow, black, and white finch. A resident of the north woods, Evening Grosbeaks undergo an occasional "irruption", when larger than normal numbers move south during the winter in search of food. In the past, these irruptions happened every few years. In 1984, nearly 2,700 were counted statewide during the Christmas Bird Count. Sadly, following large population declines, they have become a scarce winter visitor in Ohio between November and April. Now only a handful show up each winter, if any. When they do show up, they are generally found at bird feeders where their large bills specialize in cracking open sunflower seeds. Flocks are often vocal giving sweet, piercing calls.

Large finch with thick conical bill and yellow eyebrow. Black and yellow overall with prominent white wing patches. Female/immature mostly gray with black and white wings. Neck and flanks have a touch of greenish-yellow.

American Pipit

Anthus rubescens

L 6" | **WS** 11"

Inhabiting barren habitats such as agricultural fields, shore-lines, mudflats, and expansive grassy areas, the inconspicuous American Pipit is often not detected until it moves. Rather than hopping like most songbirds, American Pipits walk, typically with a chickenlike gait. They are regularly seen mixed with other ground-dwelling species such as Horned Larks and Snow Buntings in search of seeds and insects. A breeder of high-montane meadows and the arctic tundra, in Ohio they occur during spring and fall migration and regularly overwinter between September and May. Knowledge of their *pip-it!* call helps one find this rather uncommon species. Compare their call to Horned Lark, which can sound similar to the untrained ear.

In winter, birds are grayish brown above and paler below with dark streaking. Bill is short and thin, eyebrow and eyering pale. In summer (not pictured), fewer streaks if any against a more peach-colored breast and face.

Lapland Longspur

Calcarius lapponicus

L 6" | **WS** 10"

The Lapland Longspur is an uncommon winter visitor in Ohio between October and early May in open country, especially agricultural fields and road verges. Typically in flocks, they often join other open country species including Horned Larks and Snow Buntings feeding on seed between corn stubble. Their nervousness is often apparent as flocks will frequently take flight, circle around, eventually landing again to feed. When snow is not present, they blend very well into their background and are often only detected overhead when they give their distinctive short musical rattles. Lapland Longspurs migrate to the far northern tundra to breed, where they are sometimes the only songbird present.

Sparrow-like chunky bird. In winter, non-breeding adult heavily streaked above with an unmarked rusty nape. Note the black bordering around cheeks. Wings show rusty coloration. Immature birds much paler. In spring adult male (inset) molts into breeding plumage with a black crown, face, and bib, obvious rusty nape, and yellow bill.

Snow Bunting
Plectrophenax nivalis

L 6"   **WS** 12"

Few birds embody winter more than the Snow Bunting. This uncommon winter visitor inhabits barren agricultural lands, sandy beaches, parking lots, and road verges throughout Ohio between October and March, forming small to large flocks, often in association with Lapland Longspurs and Horned Larks. On their high arctic breeding grounds, these birds are a stunning black and white, but during the winter, they develop a rusty wash on their head, breast and mantle. Over the last few decades, this species has declined roughly 50 percent but is still reliably found at places including the Lake Erie coastline and rural farm roads, especially in Amish communities. Listen for their clear *tew* in flight.

In flight, very distinctive with extensive white in the wings and tail.

Compact yellow billed sparrow-like bird. In winter, male and female are a combination of rust, black, and white in plumage with males paler overall. Male has rusty ear patch and shoulders; female tends to be rust-colored throughout the head and breast.

Chipping Sparrow

Spizella passerina

L 5" | **WS** 8"

The Chipping Sparrow is a widespread breeder across Ohio, feeding on grassy lawns and nesting in ornamental shrubs of suburban and rural neighborhoods, parks, and cemeteries. One of the most common sparrows in Ohio, Chipping Sparrows begin arriving in the state in March from their southern U.S. wintering grounds and stay through November before heading back south. A small number remain through the winter mainly in urban metro areas especially in Columbus, Dayton, and Cincinnati. Their song is commonly heard throughout the spring and summer and is characterized by a long dry trill of evenly spaced chips. They also give a variety of single chip notes.

Small and slim. Adult in summer has bright rusty crown, black eyeline, and unstreaked grayish underparts.

Juvenile has heavily streaked underparts and streaked brown crown.

In winter, adult paler with brownish crown, not rusty. Note dark eyeline and unstreaked grayish underparts.

Clay-colored Sparrow

Spizella pallida

L 5" | **WS** 8"

The Clay-colored Sparrow is a common and widespread species of the Great Plains. In Ohio it is a scarce migrant because the state lies just east of the migration route. A few turn up every year, mostly along Lake Erie but inland as well. Scrutiny is needed to distinguish them from the similar Chipping Sparrow. Look for their gray nape and contrasting facial pattern. Clay-colored Sparrows have expanded their range eastward as their preferred open shrubby habitat has increased. In 1998, Ohio confirmed the first nesting attempt of this species at Battelle Darby Creek Metro Park in Columbus. In 2008, a hybrid Clay-colored and Field Sparrow was discovered in Lorain County.

Small slender sparrow resembling Chipping Sparrow but has gray nape and contrasting facial pattern including a pale moustache.

Field Sparrow
Spizella pusilla

L 6" | **WS** 8"

The plaintive whistled song of the Field Sparrow, often described like a bouncing ping-pong ball, is a common song throughout Ohio in spring and summer. Contrary to the name, Field Sparrows prefer a variety of shrubby, second-growth habitats, where they perch atop a fence row or tall shrub to sing. Present year-round, their numbers are highest from April to October when migrants from the south have joined our residents and are in full song. In winter, Field Sparrows are unobtrusive, quietly feeding in small flocks on the ground and retreating into shrubs when disturbed.

Small, slender, long-tailed sparrow with a gray face and distinctive eyering, rusty crown and eye patch, and orange conical bill. Back and wings are rust-colored with two white wing bars.

Lark Sparrow

Chondestes grammacus

L 6" | **WS** 11"

The Lark Sparrow reaches its easternmost breeding range within Ohio, where it is highly localized. Their breeding habitat is characterized by sparsely vegetated fields and hillside pastures. In the 1860s, Lark Sparrows expanded their range eastward with the clearing of forests, and by the 1930s, they were confirmed breeding in 39 of Ohio's counties. As land use changed and converted to housing complexes, their range retreated westward again with only a few populations remaining in the state. The Lark Sparrow is now a state endangered species. The vegetated sandy beach ridges of Oak Openings Metro Park near Toledo hold the state's largest population and are your best bet for finding this rare breeder. Most other summering birds are found between Dayton and Cincinnati, most notably at Oakes Quarry Park near Dayton. Aside from the odd winter records, they are mostly present between April and July when their melodious song of various notes and trills interspersed with harsh buzzes can be heard.

A larger sparrow with boldly marked head pattern, chestnut crown, and black spot on otherwise pale breast.

American Tree Sparrow

Spizelloides arborea

L 6"   **WS** 10"

The hardy American Tree Sparrow is one of the most northern breeding and wintering species of sparrow in North America. Come October, small flocks can be found in open country throughout the state including open fields, woodland edges, backyards, and shrubby road verges. During the winter, American Tree Sparrows typically feed on the ground, under feeders, and along roadsides where they feed primarily on seeds. Their *teel-it* contact call is often heard. By the end of April, most of the population will have left Ohio for their northern Canadian breeding grounds, though a few lingering individuals may be seen well into May.

Richly colored above and plain unstreaked below with a central dark spot on breast. Gray face complemented by a rusty cap and eye stripe and bicolored bill.

Fox Sparrow

Passerella iliaca

L 7" | **WS** 10"

The big chunky Fox Sparrow is an uncommon to locally common migrant and winter visitor to Ohio, where they occur in shrubby thickets, undergrowth, woodland edges, and occasionally backyard bird feeders. They are present from October to early May with a slight uptick in numbers from late March to early April, when larger numbers begin to concentrate along Lake Erie. Watch for them foraging on the ground where they kick up leaf litter in search of food. Western populations are variable gray to dark brown, but in Ohio they are foxy red. Mostly quiet, the Fox Sparrow will occasionally give a sharp repeated *chu* or a piercing *sip* call.

Large and chunky. Eastern populations reddish-brown with dense streaking. Face is gray and bill black and yellow

Heavily spotted underparts typically with a large central spot on the breast.

Dark-eyed Junco

Junco hyemalis

L 6"   **WS** 9"

The arrival of Dark-eyed Juncos in the fall represents the arrival of winter and colder temperatures. Nicknamed "snow-birds," juncos are common to abundant throughout Ohio from October to April in conifer and mixed woodlands, thickets, woodland edges, and suburban areas including backyard bird feeders. These energetic sparrows feed on the ground by hopping and flashing their white outer tail feathers while scratching at the ground in search of food. While most depart the state by the end of April, the northeastern corner of the state plays host to a breeding population which favors mature hemlock gorges and mixed conifer woodlands, most notably at Cuyahoga Valley National Park, the Holden Arboretum, and the Chagrin River and Grand River corridors. Their song is similar to the trill of the Chipping Sparrow but slower and louder. More often heard is their sharp chip note, often repeated.

dult male dark slate-colored with
ontrasting white belly. Flashes white
uter tail feathers frequently. Bill
ale. Female and immature similar to
ale but typically much browner.

White-crowned Sparrow
Zonotrichia leucophrys

L 6" | **WS** 9"

The handsome White-crowned Sparrow with its striking black and white striped head is a common migrant and winter visitor throughout Ohio. In the fall they begin arriving in late September and peak through October. They occupy shrubby areas, brush piles, thickets, fencerows, and other second-growth habitats and will occasionally visit bird feeders. Although they overwinter throughout the state, the largest numbers are found in central and southern Ohio. Their northward departure in spring peaks in early May when large concentrations can be found especially along the Lake Erie coastline. One of the largest sparrows to occur in Ohio, their song is characterized by a series of whistles followed by buzzy notes.

Large grayish sparrow with distinctive black and white striped crown, often peaked. Bill mostly yellow.

Immaure like adult but crown is brown and white striped.

White-throated Sparrow

Zonotrichia albicollis

L 7" | **WS** 9"

A common migrant and winter visitor throughout Ohio from September to May, White-throated Sparrows are at home in dense underbrush of woodlands and backyards, and they regularly scratch at the ground under bird feeders for seed scraps. Even during the winter, White-throated Sparrows will sing, and to some their whistled song sounds like *oh-sweet-canada-canada-canada* while others hear *oh-sam-peabody-peabody-peabody*. They are particularly vocal in spring when larger concentrations accumulate along the Lake Erie lakefront. With their black and white striped head and white throat, they are not easily confused with any other species.

Fairly large brown sparrow with black and white crown stripes, yellow lores, and white throat patch.

Some individuals, known as "tan-striped", are less contrasting and have brown and black crown stripes, faint yellow lores, and dark bordering to white throat patch.

Harris's Sparrow

Zonotrichia querula

L 7" | **WS** 11"

The dapper Harris's Sparrow is a rare visitor to Ohio with a few showing up each winter. The only species of bird that solely breeds within Canada, they migrate south to the central Great Plains from South Dakota to Texas to spend the winter. Many individuals stray east of their typical range showing up just about anywhere in the Great Lakes region. Most often Harris's Sparrows are seen at backyard bird feeders where they associate with their close relative, the White-crowned Sparrow. Elsewhere they prefer thickets and shrubby fields. Most sightings in the state come from the western Lake Erie basin and particularly the Wayne and Holmes County Amish communities, where there is a large concentration of knowledgeable birders who tend to bird feeders throughout the winter.

Large mostly brown sparrow with white underparts. Adult has black specking on crown and a distinctive black throat and necklace with contrasting pink bill.

Immature like adult but black is limited to the necklace only.

Vesper Sparrow

Pooecetes gramineus

L 6" | **WS** 10"

A bird of wide-open country, especially large agricultural areas, Vesper Sparrows tend to be underreported because few people go birding in their breeding habitat. A proper "LBJ" (little brown job), Vesper Sparrows are nondescript and are best told by their white eye ring and musical song of several whistles followed by rising and falling notes and ending in a buzzy trill. Uncommon throughout the state, they are mostly absent as breeders in south-central and eastern Ohio and are more common in the western half of the state where more desirable habitat can be found. Watch for them feeding along road verges next to crop fields between March and October, though a few have been found overwintering.

A medium to large nondescript sparrow. Note the prominent white eye ring and white outer-tail feathers.

Savannah Sparrow

Passerculus sandwichensis

L 5" | **WS** 8"

The Savannah Sparrow is a widespread species found in grass-lands, open meadows, agricultural fields, and pastures. Rare in winter, they are most common in the state from April to October avoiding much of the mature forests of southeastern Ohio. Their song, consisting of a couple of tick notes followed by an insect-like trill, is often given conspicuously from a prominent perch such as a fencepost or tall weed. Their name appears to confirm their preference for grassland, or savanna, but they were named after a specimen collected near Savannah, Georgia.

Medium-sized sparrow with fairly small bill, yellow lores, and strong facial pattern. Streaking on breast converge into a central dark spot.

Henslow's Sparrow

Centronyx henslowii

L 5" | **WS** 7"

The inconspicuous Henslow's Sparrow is an uncommon summer breeding resident in Ohio between May and August with some lingering well into October. Unlike the more prevalent Grasshopper and Savannah Sparrows, Henslow's prefer extensive tall, dense grasslands. Having suffered widespread population declines over the last half-century due to the degradation of grasslands across their range, the extensive reclaimed strip mines of eastern Ohio have helped their population at a local level. The Wilds, Tri-River and Crown City Wildlife Areas, Battelle Darby Creek Metro Park, Glacier Ridge Metro Park, Bath Nature Reserve, and Oak Openings Preserve Metro Park are all excellent places to find this species. Listen for their unimpressive *hiccup* song lasting less than a second, typically from an obscured perch.

Large flat head with olive-green wash to face. Black markings behind and below the eye. Thick bill. Upperparts marked with broad dark stripes, and breast has small blotches. Tail is short and spiky.

Grasshopper Sparrow

Ammodramus savannarum

L 5"   **WS** 8"

The small inconspicuous Grasshopper Sparrow inhabits dry upland habitats of tall grassland, hayfields, fields bordering airports, and reclaimed strip mines. Almost always detected first by song, Grasshopper Sparrows produce an insect-like *tick-tick-tzzzzz* typically from a tall blade of grass or plant. As with numerous grassland species, Grasshopper Sparrows have been on the decline. The conversion of grasslands to croplands and more frequent mowing of hayfields are to blame. Fortunately, the reclaimed strip mines of eastern Ohio helped to compensate for some of this decline, especially around The Wilds southeast of Zanesville. Migrants and breeding residents are present in the state from April to August with some individuals staying well into October. Breeding occurs throughout the state, though less frequently in the northeastern corner and the mostly forested southern region of the state.

Small, flat-headed sparrow with unstreaked buffy underparts and rusty streaking on back. Note yellow spot in front of eyes and yellow shoulder patch which is often visible.

Song Sparrow

Melospiza melodia

L 6" | **WS** 9"

The Song Sparrow is not only the most common sparrow in Ohio, but one of the most common and widespread species of bird in the state. Year-round residents, Song Sparrows will nest in virtually any habitat except barren fields and mature woodlands. They especially like shrubby thickets, brushy fencerows, undergrowth, and roadside scrub. The song is characterized by several clear introductory notes followed by a varied melodious warble. Peak breeding is between April and August when some pairs can have as many as three broods. Occasionally Song Sparrows will show up under your feeders, where they scratch the ground with their feet in search of seeds.

Medium-sized long-tailed, round-headed, coarsely streaked sparrow with a central dark spot on breast. Malar and mustache broadly striped.

Lincoln's Sparrow
Melospiza lincolnii

L 6" | **WS** 8"

The secretive Lincoln's Sparrow rarely ventures far from cover as it feeds in brushy fields and thickets. Solely a migrant throughout Ohio, during the spring Lincoln's Sparrows pass through from late April through May and again in the fall between September and early November. It may come as a surprise that the Lincoln's Sparrow was not named for Abraham Lincoln, but instead John James Audubon's companion during an exploration in Quebec. James Lincoln was the only person who was able to collect a specimen for study.

Elegant and finely marked as with a sharpened pencil. Gray face, small bill, pale eye ring, and buffy coloration on malar and chest.

Crisp markings on buffy breast. Underparts white. Crown often peaked when alert.

Swamp Sparrow
Melospiza georgiana

L 5"   **WS** 7"

As their name suggests, Swamp Sparrows occur in shrubby swamps, brushy margins of ponds and lakes, as well as cattail marshes and wet meadows. In winter, they can be found throughout the state, but during the summer, the majority breed north and east of Columbus avoiding much of southern and western regions of the state. Often heard before seen, Swamp Sparrows sing a musical liquid trill slower than Chipping Sparrow. Most wetlands in northeastern Ohio host this common but at times elusive species. The long legs of the Swamp Sparrow are an adaptation for wading in shallow water, and occasionally they dip their head in to catch aquatic insects.

Medium-sized sparrow with gray face, nape, and breast, rusty cap, and reddish-brown wings.

Eastern Towhee
Pipilo erythrophthalmus

L 8" | **WS** 10"

The attractive Eastern Towhee is named for its call, a two-note
che-wink, often repeated from brushy or shrubby undergrowth,
tangles, and overgrown fields. More familiar is their song, a
three syllabled *drink-your-tea*, the last note ending
in a short trill. Eastern Towhees are common to abundant residents throughout Ohio and occur throughout the year.
They are especially abundant in southern and eastern Ohio
in the unglaciated Appalachian foothills and tend to be localized in extreme northwestern Ohio. During the winter, they
disappear from some areas in northern Ohio avoiding the cold
weather. With their larger size and striking colors, one might
not realize that Eastern Towhees are actually part of
the sparrow family and spend much of their time scratching
at the ground in search of food.

Oversized sparrow with
black upperparts, head, and
breast, white belly, and
rufous flanks. Tail is long and
black with white corners.

Female very much like the
male but black is replaced
with brown.

Yellow-breasted Chat

Icteria virens

L 7" | **WS** 10"

Once believed to be a type of warbler, the much larger Yellow-breasted Chat was placed in its own family in 2017. They occur in dense vegetation, including shrubby habitat along ponds and wetlands, overgrown brushy fields, and thickets, and they can be quite elusive. Their large repertoire of whistles, rattles, chatters, and gurgles often give away their location. Present from mid-April through September, Yellow-breasted Chats have a statewide distribution but are more common in the southern half of the state. Some regions of northern Ohio, especially in the northwest, can be void of chats except during migration.

Size of large sparrow, olive green above with white spectacles, a yellow breast, and white underparts. Furtive, thicket-loving behavior typical.

Yellow-headed Blackbird

Xanthocephalus xanthocephalus

L 9" | **WS** 17"

The distinctive and aptly named Yellow-headed Blackbird is a rare local breeder in Ohio, which is at the eastern edge of the range. Howard Marsh Metro Park, Metzger Marsh Wildlife Area, and Ottawa National Wildlife Refuge in the western Lake Erie basin hold most if not all the breeding population in the state, which numbers only a handful of pairs. Here they prefer extensive marshes dominated by cattail and other tall emergent vegetation. Outside of summer, Yellow-headed Blackbirds are accidental to rare but can show up just about anywhere, especially in the western portion of the state, along Lake Erie, and around the Akron, Canton, and Wooster region of northeastern Ohio. Their song ranks high as one of the most bizarre sounds in the bird world, a shrieking buzz lasting several seconds.

Distinctive large blackbird with a yellow head and breast sharply contrasting with black body. White wing patch visible at rest.

Male in flight displaying extensive white wing patch.

Female all brown with duller yellow on head and breast.

Bobolink

Dolichonyx oryzivorus

L 7" | **WS** 11"

The bubbly metallic song of the Bobolink is a sign of spring when these blackbirds display over hayfields, grasslands, and pastures throughout the state. Present from April to October, some Bobolinks travel up to 12,000 miles to and from South America each year to breed. As true with many other grassland species, the Bobolink has undergone large population declines due to hayfields being cut more frequently or converted to crop fields. Although mostly absent from southeastern Ohio's mostly forested unglaciated region, the reclaimed strip mines in the area offered new breeding sites for this declining species. The Wilds is an excellent example of this success.

Breeding male black below and black and white above with a black head, golden nape, and black bill.

Female and nonbreeding male warm brown below with faint streaking on flanks. Upperparts darker, crown striped black, bill pale, and thin black line through eye.

Eastern Meadowlark

Sturnella magna

L 9" | **WS** 15"

The whistled *spring-is-here* song of the Eastern Meadowlark is commonly heard throughout Ohio's grasslands, hayfields, pastures, and reclaimed strip mines during the spring and summer. Although their numbers have declined over the years as grasslands and hayfields were converted to croplands, they remain a common and widespread resident in the state. Present year-round, they are most common from April to October during the breeding season when residents are joined by migrants from farther south. The name suggests a lark, but meadowlarks are part of the blackbird family.

Medium-sized chunky songbird. Underparts yellow with a black V on chest. Flanks and upperparts streaked brown. Head flat with long bill.

Orchard Oriole

Icterus spurius

L 7" | **WS** 10"

The lesser-known of our two species of Ohio orioles, the Orchard is a summer breeding resident only. Arriving in late April, they occur statewide in second-growth and forest-edge habitats including fields with scattered trees, riparian corridors, fencerows, and shrubby thickets. Their loud, clear whistled song interspersed with harsh chatters often brings attention to their presence, but is often not recognized right away. Orchard Orioles tend to head south earlier than most migrant songbirds, with the majority departing the state by the end of August.

Small and slender. Adult male is mostly black above with chestnut underparts and chestnut wing patch.

Immature male like female but has a black throat.

Female greenish-yellow overall with two wing bars and sharply pointed bill.

Baltimore Oriole

Icterus galbula

L 7" | **WS** 11"

The eye-catching Baltimore Oriole is a common summer breeding
resident throughout Ohio. This member of the blackbird family
may be found in open woodlands and large shade trees, especially
near a stream, pond, or lake. Starting in late April, Baltimore
Orioles can be heard from the treetops giving their territorial
loud, clear whistles and chatters. Closer views can be obtained by
slicing an orange in half and placing the halves at eye level onto
branches or hooks. Grape jelly is another option, and orioles will
also feed from hummingbird feeders. Baltimore Orioles head
south to their Central American wintering grounds by the end
of September.

Adult male stunning orange
underparts with a black head
and back, orange shoulders
and rump, and white
markings on black wings.

mmature female dull lacking any black. Head, breast, and undertail coverts washed yellow. Back and wings gray. Tail yellow.

Adult female variable. Yellow to orange overall with brownish heads and backs. Overall less colorful than the male. Note the orange tail.

Red-winged Blackbird

Agelaius phoeniceus

L 9" | **WS** 14"

One of the most abundant and recognized songbirds in Ohio, the Red-winged Blackbird occupies open habitats including marshes, roadside ditches, pastures, and hayfields. Their lively *konk-ah-ree!* song is a sure sign of spring, even though many overwinter throughout Ohio every year. The males are commonly seen perched on a tree, fence post, or other prominent perches to sing while flashing their iconic red epaulets, or shoulder patches. Females, on the other hand, resemble large sparrows and are often misidentified by those just learning bird identification. Breeding season typically runs from late April to July when the polygamous males will mate with multiple females, which nest in woven cups made from grass hung from tall herbaceous vegetation. Outside of breeding season, Red-winged Blackbirds flock together, often with other blackbird species, and can number in the tens of thousands.

Breeding male entirely black with a red shoulder patch bordered by yellow.

In winter, males can look scaly with limited red in the shoulders visible.

Female nondescript brown and heavily streaked throughout with a hint of yellow wash around the bill. Resembles a large sparrow to the untrained eye.

Brown-headed Cowbird

Molothrus ater

L 7" | **WS** 12"

Love them or hate them, the Brown-headed Cowbird is here
to stay. This parasitic species is responsible for laying eggs in
other birds' nests. The offspring out-compete the host species'
young, and the host parents typically end up rearing the
cowbird chicks. This is a natural occurrence in the ecosystem
dating back to when large herds of bison roamed North
America. Brown-headed Cowbirds probably followed these
herds without enough time to build nests and raise young
before the herd continued, so females resorted to laying their
eggs in other birds' nests in order to keep up with the herds.
Originally cowbirds were probably present in Ohio in small
numbers prior to the mid-1800s but with the removal of forests,
they expanded their range into these open habitats they
prefer. This is a native species, and it, the nest, and the eggs
are protected. Unlike other blackbirds, the cowbird's song is a
liquid gurgle followed by a whistle.

Female nondescript
plain brown overall with
very faint streaking on
underparts. Eye is black

Adult male entirely black with an all brown head.

Juvenile (seen here being fed by a Chipping Sparrow) is brown overall with a scaly-looking back and streaked underparts

Rusty Blackbird

Euphagus carolinus

L 9" | **WS** 14"

The Rusty Blackbird is the most northern breeding blackbird in North America, where it nests in spruce bogs, wet woods, and beaver ponds of Canada, Alaska, and the northeastern tier of the U.S. In Ohio we see this winter visitor from September through April where they are often mixed with large blackbird and grackle flocks or in small numbers in wetlands and flooded woodlands. The greatest numbers occur in Ohio during migration from April to May and October to November. Due to the destruction of wetland habitat across their wintering range, among other factors, the Rusty Blackbird has seen a decline of 90 percent in the past half-century, one of the largest declines of any species in North America. They are most often found in northeastern Ohio and the western Lake Erie basin including Ottawa National Wildlife Refuge, but they can be seen just about anywhere in the state.

Breeding adult all glossy black with a greenish sheen evident in certain lighting.

Winter male variable. Some are dark overall with rusty edging to feathers and paler eye and eyebrow. Others (pictured) have more extensive rusty tipped feathering. Note the dark eye patch.

Winter adult female brownish in color. Dark eye patch contrasts with paler supercilium and pale eye.

Common Grackle

Quiscalus quiscula

L 12" | **WS** 16"

The Common Grackle is the largest and longest-tailed black-bird in Ohio and is one of the most abundant and widespread species in the state. From flooded open woodlands to parks, cemeteries, and suburban backyards, grackles are right at home near humans. Nests are most frequently constructed in conifers and smaller trees near houses. During migration and winter, grackles are highly gregarious and flock together frequently with other blackbird species numbering up to tens of thousands. Grackles will also visit backyard bird feeders, where they can eat more than the provider would prefer. Although a year-round resident, they are most abundant between March and October, when they are most vocal. Both male and female will give a guttural *reada-eek* often with clear whistles. Their call is a short, harsh *chik*, harsher than other blackbirds.

In flight, long tail is keel-shaped. Often flocks in large numbers and mixed with other blackbird species.

Adult male (pictured) large and long-tailed. Dark overall, often bronzy, with a purplish head, pale eyes, and large bill. Female like male, but less glossy.

Ovenbird

Seiurus aurocapilla

L 5" | **WS** 9"

The Ovenbird resembles and behaves more like a member of the thrush family than the warbler family that it belongs to. This denizen of mature woodland spends much of its time on the ground foraging for food and singing its conspicuous *teacher, teacher, teacher, teacher* song. They even build their nest on the ground, shaped like a Dutch oven, hence their name. Migrants begin arriving in mid-April and can turn up anywhere in the state. During the breeding season, Ovenbirds are most common in the unglaciated southeastern Ohio where mature woodlands are predominant. They are also common around northeastern Ohio and a few scattered areas in the western regions of the state, namely Oak Openings Metro Park and other parks and reserves with extensive forest in a mostly agricultural area. Most migrant and resident Ovenbirds will depart the state by mid-October.

Small, chunky, and ground dwelling. Olive above with extensive black streaking on otherwise white underparts. Pale eye ring and crown striped black and orange.

Louisiana Waterthrush
Parkesia motacilla

L 6" | **WS** 10"

The Louisiana Waterthrush is one of the earliest spring migrants to return to Ohio, often as early as mid-March. This large warbler inhabits flowing rocky streams where it feeds along the margins bobbing its tail continuously. Spring and early summer is an excellent time to hear their song which comprises several clear descending whistles followed by a melodic jumble. Ohio lies at the northern edge of their breeding range with the unglaciated hills of southeastern Ohio holding the largest concentration. Elsewhere they are widespread with decent numbers in the northeastern, central, and southwestern regions of the state, although avoiding the northwestern corner. Fall migration begins as early as July, although a few linger in the state into August and September. Compare these to the similar Northern Waterthrush.

A thrush-like warbler with long legs and white eyebrow stripe becoming wider at the rear. Pale underparts streaked.

Northern Waterthrush

Parkesia noveboracensis

L 5" | **WS** 9"

The Northern Waterthrush is a common migrant and rare breeder in Ohio. By the time Northern migrates through in spring, between mid-April through May, most Louisiana Waterthrushes will already be on territory. The breeding population of Northern in the state is restricted to the far northeastern corner, and they remain quite scarce occupying flooded woodlands and brushy swamps, bogs, and quiet streams. Listen for their loud abrupt song *sweet sweet sweet swee wee wee chew chew chew* by spring migrants and breeding individuals alike. Fall migration begins in late August and extends to early October with some individuals lingering through November. Compare to the similar Louisiana Waterthrush.

Like Louisiana Waterthrush but eyebrow buffy, not white, and more heavily streaked below. Some individuals have a more extensive yellow wash below.

Worm-eating Warbler

Helmitheros vermivorum

L 5" | **WS** 9"

The Worm-eating Warbler is one of the more southern breeding warblers in North America and inhabits well wooded hillsides with a dense understory. It is no surprise that the vast majority breed in south-central Ohio's Appalachian foothills. These inconspicuous warblers begin arriving late April and are rare migrants away from their breeding sites. The occasional individual will overshoot the breeding grounds appearing well north of the range, especially along Lake Erie. Shawnee, Mohican and Zaleski State Forests, Wayne National Forest, Conkle's Hollow State Nature Preserve, and Clear Creek Metro Park host the majority of the state's breeding birds, with Mohican the most northern population. In spring listen for their dry, insect-like trill. They are hard to detect by the end of July, though some will linger until early October.

Olive-brown above and buffy below with prominent black head stripes.

Golden-winged Warbler

Vermivora chrysoptera

L 5 " | **WS** 9 "

The splendid Golden-winged Warbler is arguably one of the most striking and highly sought-after species of warbler in Ohio. Once more widespread in the state, with the expansion of the closely related Blue-winged Warbler, maturing of forests, and habitat loss, the Golden-winged Warbler is rapidly declining. Spring migrants typically move through during the first three weeks of May and can turn up just about anywhere in the state. The Lake Erie coastline probably offers your best chance at finding one. Listen for their *bee buzz buzz* song, but take care because Blue-winged and Golden-winged Warblers often sing each other's song, which is no surprise as these two species regularly hybridize. Golden-winged formerly bred in Ohio, but sadly hasn't in recent years. Fall migrants typically pass through during September.

Male striking. Gray overall with golden shoulders and cap and a black throat and mask.

Female similar to male but black face and throat replaced with gray.

Blue-winged Warbler

Vermivora cyanoptera

L 5" | **WS** 7"

The *bee-buzzz* song of the Blue-winged Warbler is unmistakable in overgrown fields, woodland clearings, and other second-growth habitats during the spring and summer. Historically, Blue-winged Warblers were probably absent from Ohio and the rest of the Great Lakes region until European settlers arrived and cleared land creating more desirable habitat. In recent years, however, forests have been maturing and their numbers have declined. They are still fairly common migrants and breeding residents throughout Ohio, with most of the breeding population in the eastern half of the state. Very few breed in western and northwestern Ohio aside from Oak Openings Metro Park. Most depart the state by the end of September or early October. A close relative to the Golden-winged Warbler, these two species regularly hybridize.

All yellow with gray wings and black thin bill. Adult male has two wing bars and a black eyeline. Female similar to male but eyeline grayer and crown more olive than yellow. Hybrids between Blue-winged and Golden-winged Warblers occur, called "Brewster's" and "Lawrence's" depending on characteristics. The hybrids share field marks of both species. Brewster's (inset) is more regularly found, while Lawrence's is scarce.

Black-and-white Warbler

Mniotilta varia

L 5" | **WS** 8"

The aptly named Black-and-white Warbler is unique among the warblers as it creeps along tree trunks and branches much like a creeper or nuthatch. In a family full of colors, this pied bird is no less striking. A common migrant, spring migration peaks from late April through May when they can be found state-wide singly or mixed with other migrant warblers. A locally common to uncommon breeding resident, Black-and-white Warblers prefer second-growth to mature woodlands mainly in southern and eastern Ohio but do breed throughout. Often their "squeaky-wheel" song alerts you to their presence. Fall migration begins in late August and lasts through mid-October.

Male unmistakable. Striped black and white all over. Female (inset) a duller version of male, lacks the black on the throat and has a grayish, not black, ear patch.

Prothonotary Warbler

Protonotaria citrea

L 5.5" | **WS** 8.75"

The Prothonotary Warbler, nicknamed the "Golden Swamp Warbler" for its preference for woody swamps, is Ohio's only cavity-nesting warbler. Present from mid-April through September, this southern species produces a loud monotone *sweet sweet sweet sweet* song on territory. Although declining due to habitat loss, they are fairly widespread throughout Ohio and can be locally common, especially where man-made nesting boxes have been erected. Some reliable sites for this species include Magee Marsh Wildlife Area and Ottawa National Wildlife Refuge in northwest Ohio, Mosquito Lake and Berlin Lake in northeast Ohio, Hoover Reservoir in Columbus, and East Fork State Park in southwest Ohio. The name "Prothonotary" refers to the yellow robes worn by clerks in the Catholic Church.

Fairly large mostly yellow warbler with an olive back, gray wings, and white undertail coverts. Female (not pictured) tends to be paler with a more greenish wash to crown and nape. Note the large black bill.

Orange-crowned Warbler

Oreothlypis celata

L 5" **WS** 7"

Orange-crowned Warblers won't be winning any awards for most colorful warbler, but their scarcity in the state makes them just as exciting. More common in the western U.S., these warblers pass through Ohio in small numbers during the spring from mid-April to mid-May, typically staying fairly low in shrubs. You may wonder where their orange crown is, but this feature is typically hidden and only visible when the bird is excited or alert. Southbound migration occurs through September and October, when Orange-crowned Warblers have a fondness for goldenrod-laden shrubby fields.

Small with a thin, pointy bill. Some individuals yellow-green overall lacking any features. They are distinguished from Tennessee by their yellow, not white, undertail coverts and faint streaking on breast. Other individuals (inset) can be quite gray overall but still have diagnostic yellow undertail coverts.

Tennessee Warbler

Oreothlypis peregrina

L 5" | **WS** 8"

The dainty Tennessee Warbler winters in Central and South America where they often utilize shade coffee plantations, further proving the importance of shade vs. conventional coffee plantations. Their breeding range extends across the northern boreal forests of Canada and extreme northern U.S. where they specialize in eating spruce budworm caterpillars. In Ohio, we see this common migrant during the spring and fall where they often feed in the canopy of large shade trees. In the spring Tennessee Warblers move through from late April to the end of May, often later than other species. Their song begins with a staccato series of short notes followed by a series of loud, uniform chips. Fall migrants are silent and pass through from late August through October. Contrary to their name, they don't breed in Tennessee; the name happens to be where they were first described in 1811.

Small drab warbler with thin, pointy bill. Breeding male yellow-green above and plain white below with no wing bars. Head is gray with a pale eyebrow and faint dark eye line.

In fall adult and immature yellow-green overall lacking any distinct wing bars, Note the thin bill and white undertail coverts.

Breeding female like male but usually more yellow-green below. Gray on head is typically limited to the cap.

Nashville Warbler

Oreothlypis ruficapilla

L 4" | **WS** 7"

The Nashville Warbler is a common spring and fall migrant in Ohio, especially during the first half of May. It does not breed near Nashville, Tennessee, but ornithologist Alexander Wilson first discovered it there in 1811. Instead, Nashville Warblers breed in Canada and the northern U.S. Although unexpected, they have bred in Ohio at least three times. Their song begins with several paired notes, the first one higher, followed by a rapid, even trill, similar to Tennessee Warbler but sweeter. Sometimes confused with the scarce Connecticut Warbler, Nashville is much smaller, has a yellow throat and most often feeds in tree canopies. Connecticuts are almost always seen on or near the ground.

One of the smallest warblers. Upperparts olive-green and underparts yellow. Head gray with a bold white eye ring and yellow throat. Male has a chestnut crown patch that's not always visible. Female and immature similar but duller overall.

Connecticut Warbler

Oporornis agilis

L 5-6" | **WS** 9"

Uncommon, quiet, and secretive, the Connecticut Warbler ranks high as one of the most sought-after warblers in Ohio. In spring, they pass through later than other migrants and are typically found during the second half of May. Connecticuts can turn up anywhere in the state, and urban metro parks and the Lake Erie coastline are excellent places to search. Your best chance to find this elusive warbler is by searching in early morning as males will sing at dawn and go silent shortly after. Scan the ground as they spend much of their time walking sluggishly under dense undergrowth, occasionally hopping up onto a low branch. If you see one high in a tree, you're probably looking at a Nashville Warbler, which also has a yellow throat. In fall, Connecticuts migrate early, most passing through during the last three weeks of September.

Large and sturdy warbler with a uniform olive-green back, yellow underparts, gray hood, and complete eye ring. Note gray hood extends down to the chest. Similar Nashville is smaller with a yellow throat. Female and immature hood more brown and less contrasting.

Mourning Warbler

Geothlypis philadelphia

L 5" | **WS** 7"

The Mourning Warbler is one of the latest warblers to migrate through Ohio in the spring, typically from mid-May to early June. Like Connecticut, Mournings can be elusive and hard to see as they feed on the ground under thickets. Fortunately, they are somewhat more common than Connecticut and often sing their loud musical *churee, churee, churee, turtle* song early in the morning. A very rare breeder in second-growth habitats, historically they bred in several areas in northern Ohio including Oak Openings Metro Park. Lately, there have been very few summering birds, although probable breeders have been found in Ashtabula and Trumbull County in recent years. Most fall migrants are found from late August through September, and a few are seen into October.

Male olive-green above and yellow below with a gray hood and black chest. Note the lack of an eye ring unlike Nashville and Conecticut Warbler. Female has duller hood and lacks the black chest. Juvenile, seen in the fall, often lacks gray on the chest and has pale broken eye ring.

Kentucky Warbler

Geothlypis formosus

L 5" | **WS** 8"

Ohio is at the northern limit of the Kentucky Warbler's range, where it is an uncommon breeding resident throughout southern Ohio as far north as Dayton, Columbus, Mansfield, and Canton. Present from late April through October, they occupy understory of mature deciduous woodlands typically avoiding forest edge and smaller woodlots. In spring, males sing relentlessly a loud *churry, churry, churry* often when concealed in the understory. Reliable places for this species include East Fork State Park, Shawnee and Zaleski State Forests, Wayne National Forest, Clear Creek Metro Park, and Mohican State Park, to name a few.

Medium-sized and long-legged. Adult male olive-green above and yellow below with black sideburns and crown. Female (not shown) sideburns tend to be smaller and grayer.

Common Yellowthroat

Geothlypis trichas

L 5" | **WS** 7"

The loud *witchity-witchity-witchity-witchity* song of the
Common Yellowthroat is regularly heard from the margins of
marshes and ponds, wet meadows, and brushy fields. One of
the most abundant warblers in Ohio, yellowthroats occur
statewide from mid-April through October, and a few regularly linger into winter. Watch for yellowthroats skulking in
cattails or dense thickets as they search for food, particularly
insects and spiders. Males, aka "masked bandits," are unmistakable with their black masks. Females are less easy to identify
without the mask.

Grayish-brown overall
with yellow throat and
undertail coverts. Male
has distinctive black mask

Female and immature
lack the black mask, but
instead have a grayish
face. Note the bright
yellow throat.

Hooded Warbler

Setophaga citrina

L 5" | **WS** 8"

A warbler of mature woodlands with a good understory, the Hooded Warbler is a common breeder in the eastern U.S. including Ohio. Beginning in April, the *weeto, weeto, weet-ee-oh* song of male Hooded Warblers defending their territories are conspicuous throughout southern and eastern Ohio. In western Ohio's mostly agricultural landscape, Hooded Warblers only appear in early spring during migration aside from a few pockets of breeding birds including Oak Openings Metro Park near Toledo. These forest specialties spend much of their time at eye-level where they actively feed, while flashing white spots on their outer tail feathers. Through October, their numbers taper off as they head south to their wintering grounds in the Caribbean, Mexico, and Central America.

Adult male olive green above, yellow below with a yellow face and black hood and throat. Often flicks outer tail which reveals white outer tail feathers.

Female and immature show little to no hood. Otherwise entirely yellow with an olive-green back and white outer tail feathers.

American Redstart

Setophaga ruticilla

L 5" | **WS** 7"

Energetic and acrobatic, American Redstarts dash around
from branch to branch scaring up insects by drooping their
wings and flicking their colorful tails. An abundant migrant
and locally common summer breeder, in spring redstarts pass
through between late April and May while residents remain in
deciduous woodlands to breed. Mostly absent from the western
half of Ohio during the summer, American Redstarts are especially common in the northeast. Numbers increase again during
fall migration from late August to mid-October.

Adult male unmistakable.
Mostly black with
orange patches on
wings, sides, and tail.

Female similarly patterned to male but back
olive, head gray, and underparts pale with
yellow patches on wings, sides, and tail.
Immature male very similar to female but has a
variable amount of black smudges on head and
breast.

Kirtland's Warbler

Setophaga kirtlandii

L 5.75" | **WS** 8.75"

Few birds get birders' adrenaline pumping more than the federally endangered Kirtland's Warbler. The rare Kirtland's Warbler was first described from Cleveland, Ohio, on May 13, 1851, when Jared Kirtland found one on his father-in-law's farm. It took another 50 years before their breeding grounds were discovered in young jack pine forests of central Michigan. For the winter, they migrate to the Bahamas. It's no surprise that the first one was discovered in Ohio, because the majority of Kirtland's must travel through the state between their wintering and breeding grounds. From a record low of a couple hundred individuals in 1970s, as of 2018 more than 5,000 individuals are estimated, spread over Michigan, Wisconsin, and at least one location in Ontario. They remain a very rare migrant in Ohio from early to mid-May and from mid-September to early October. Listen for their loud, clear *chip-chip-che-way-o* song in spring. Most Ohio records come from the western Lake Erie basin at places such as Magee Marsh Wildlife Area as well as the metro parks around Columbus.

Large for a warbler. Upperparts blue-gray with dark streaks down the back. Throat and belly yellow with streaking on flanks. Note the black face and broken white eye ring. Female like male but duller yellow with no black on face.

Cape May Warbler

Setophaga tigrina

L 5" | **WS** 8"

The Cape May Warbler spends the winter soaking up the sun in the West Indies and migrates to the boreal forest of Canada and northernmost U.S. to breed. In Ohio they are a common migrant from late April through May in the spring and late August through October in the fall. Their numbers fluctuate drastically from year to year depending on outbreaks of the spruce budworm, which is their main food source on the breeding grounds. Away from the breeding grounds, Cape May Warblers are known to feed on nectar and are unique among warblers for their semi-tubular tongue which aids in collecting nectar. Excellent hearing is needed to detect their song, a series of very high-pitched *tseet* notes repeated quickly.

Short-tailed, small-headed, and very thin bill. Breeding male has distinctive chestnut cheek patch and yellow collar. Throat and underparts yellow with bold black streaks. Note large white wing patch.

Immature very dull with little to no yellow. At times can be quite confusing to identify. Note the small head, very thin bill, and faint steaking down the flanks.

Breeding female much duller than male with much less yellow and a gray face patch, not chestnut.

Cerulean Warbler

Setophaga cerula

L 4.5" | **WS** 7.75"

The striking Cerulean Warbler is a high canopy-dwelling species, so their bright color won't be of much help trying to detect them. Instead, listen for their song comprised of three buzzy notes, four quick warbles, and ending in a buzzy trill. Cerulean Warblers winter in the northern Andes of South America and breed throughout the Midwest and Appalachian Mountains. Ohio is in the heart of their breeding range and hosts to a good portion of the breeding population. Present in the state from mid-April through September, they are most common in southern and eastern Ohio where mature forests are predominant. They are mostly absent from northwestern Ohio except in migration.

Small sky-blue warbler. Upperparts blue, underparts white with blue streaks on flanks. Note the blue necklace and two white wing bars.

Female much duller and more blue-green. Underparts are slightly washed with yellow. Note the white eyebrow

Northern Parula

Setophaga americana

L 4.5" | **WS** 7"

The dainty Northern Parula is one of North America's smallest warblers. A common migrant and locally common breeder, Northern Parulas are present in Ohio from early April through October where they prefer moist hemlock, deciduous, and mixed forests. Breeding residents are most prevalent in central, south-central, and southwestern Ohio and are almost always in the tree canopy. During migration, Northern Parulas can be found throughout the state and often closer to eye level. As with many other warblers, the parula has two song types. One is characterized by a buzzy trill ending in a sharp note, almost like a little sneeze. Their alternative song is a series of rising buzzy trills with pauses in between.

Small short-tailed warbler. Adult male blue-gray above with an olive-green center on the back. Wings are blue-gray with two broad white wing bars. Throat and breast yellow with a dark chestnut band separating the two. Note the white eye crescents and black behind the bill. Adult female similar but slightly duller with less black in the face.

Immature very dull compared to adults but still shows olive-green back, yellow throat, white crescents around the eyes and two white wing bars.

Magnolia Warbler

Setophaga magnolia

L 5" | **WS** 7"

The Magnolia Warbler is one of the most common warblers that migrate through Ohio. In the spring they begin arriving in southern Ohio by late April and are widespread throughout the state during May. While most continue north for the summer, a few remain in the state to breed, mostly in the extreme north-eastern corner where they utilize hemlock gorges. They also nest farther south at Mohican State Forest and Hocking Hills State Park. Their song is a whistled *weta, weta, WETA*, the last note being the loudest. Magnolia Warblers are often known as the "field mark bird" as they have a large variety of field marks including eye line, wing bars, necklace, streaking, and mask. In the fall, they are common from late August through October.

Male has gray cap, black mask, white eye line, and yellow throat. Back is mostly black and wings have broad white wing bars. Black necklace continues down the yellow chest and belly as streaks. Note unique white tail pattern. Female similar but less striking. Immature less distinctive lacking most if not all the black streaking on the underparts

Blackburnian Warbler

Setophaga fusca

L 5" | **WS** 8"

Most Blackburnian Warblers spend the winter in the Andes of South America and migrate north to Canada, the northern U.S., and the Appalachian Mountains to breed. In spring Blackburnians move through the state from late April to the end of May, often mixing with other species of warblers. Although it is generally a canopy species, migration gives you an opportunity to see this stunning bird down low, especially at migration hotspots such as Magee Marsh. Their song is variable and nearly inaudible. Typically it begins with a series of calls rising followed by an incredibly high-pitched trill. Although a very scarce breeder in Ohio, they can be found every summer at Mohican State Forest. Blackburnian Warblers are generally one of the first northern warblers to start migrating south in the fall, and some show up as early as mid-August and continue to mid-October.

Male has fiery orange throat and face with a black crown and triangle ear patch. Back and wings black and white.

Female less colorful replacing the male's orange markings for yellow with a less contrasting face. Note the two white wing bars.

Blackpoll Warbler

Setophaga striata

L 6" | **WS** 9"

The Blackpoll Warbler undertakes the longest migration of any North American warbler between their wintering grounds in South America to their breeding grounds of Canada, Alaska, and northern New England. Some individuals travel 5,000 miles. A spruce budworm specialist, Blackpoll Warblers have a strong fondness for these moth caterpillars on their breeding grounds. In Ohio they are common spring and fall particularly from late April through May and late August through October. In spring they migrate north through the continent but in the fall, they are known to take flight off the northeast coast and undertake a 1,800-mile flight to the Caribbean or northern South America, the longest overwater flight for any songbird. The breeding plumage and wintering plumage of the Blackpoll Warbler differ drastically and could suggest that the two plumages are different species. Their song is a short series of high-pitched *tsit-tsit-tsit-tsit* notes.

Adult male mostly black and white with bright orange legs and feet. Note the black cap.

Considered a "confusing fall warbler," in fall Blackpolls are washed yellow-green overall. They can closely resemble fall Bay-breasted Warbler but note the yellow feet, not black, and faint streaking on breast, which is lacking on Bay-breasted.

Adult female not as contrasting as male and has a streaky brown cap, not black. Note the orange legs and feet.

Bay-breasted Warbler

Setophaga castanea

L 6" | **WS** 9"

The Bay-breasted Warbler is a Neotropical migrant and breeds across the vast spruce forests of Canada and northern U.S. In Ohio they are a fairly common spring migrant in May and in fall from late August through October. They turn up anywhere in the state, especially where migrants congregate along Lake Erie such as at Magee Marsh. As with other warblers that breed in the northern spruce forests, Bay-breasted Warblers specialize in eating spruce budworms and their populations can fluctuate from year to year depending on budworm outbreaks. Unlike most warblers, which tend to be energetic and always on the move, Bay-breasteds tend to be more sluggish, at times spending long periods foraging on one branch. Their song is a high-pitched *teesi, teesi, teesi.*

Large, stocky warbler with a chestnut cap, throat, and flanks. Contrasting cream-colored patch behind black face.

mature very dull. Flanks generally
ean and unstreaked usually
armly colored perhaps with a hint
chestnut. Distinguished from
ery similar fall Blackpoll Warbler
their black, not yellow, feet.

Female and fall male less
colorful but still showing
some chestnut flanks.

Chestnut-sided Warbler

Setophaga pensylvanica

L 4" | **WS** 8"

The Chestnut-sided Warbler is a common migrant in Ohio from late April through May arriving from their South American wintering grounds. During the time of John James Audubon in the early 1800s, Chestnut-sided Warblers were practically unheard of. With the clearing of mature forests, they increased in numbers following the replacement of woodlands by scrubby, second-growth habitat, which they prefer. A welcoming bird, they sing a sweet, empathetic *pleased, pleased, pleased to meetcha!* song. Summer breeders are uncommon to rare and are mostly localized to the northeastern corner of the state where they breed in forest clearings, brushy fields and thickets, and woodland edge. Fall migration begins in late August and typically ends by late October.

Male has a yellow cap, black face, yellow cheeks and diagnostic chestnut down the flanks. Wings bars are yellow.

In fall, olive-yellow cap and back, gray face, and clean underparts. Adults in nonbreeding plumage have little chestnut on flanks. Immatures have none. Note the white eye ring and yellow wing bars.

Female is like male but has a duller yellow crown and less extensive chestnut down the flanks. Face is more gray than black.

Yellow Warbler

Setophaga petechia

L 5" | **WS** 7"

The Yellow Warbler is one of the most common and widespread warblers in Ohio and across North America. Locally they begin arriving by mid-April and breed in damp brushy habitats including wetlands, ditches, and thickets of willow and alder. Their open cup nest, which is often easy to find, makes them susceptible to being parasitized by the Brown-headed Cowbird, which lays its eggs in the Yellow Warbler's nest. Some Yellow Warblers have learned to differentiate the eggs and will build a new floor in their nest on top of the cowbird egg, laying a new clutch of their own. In spring and summer their melodic *sweet, sweet, sweet, I'm so sweet!* song can be heard throughout the day. Peak breeding lasts from May through July with most birds departing by the end of September.

Male has green-yellow upperparts and bright yellow underparts with reddish streaks down the breast and belly. Female uniform yellow overall. Immature birds can appear much drabber.

Black-throated Blue Warbler

Setophaga caerulescens

L 5" | **WS** 7"

The gorgeous Black-throated Blue Warbler is a common spring and fall migrant in Ohio. They can be found in a variety of habitats including woodlands, parks, and gardens, where they typically stay low in the understory, allowing birders to avoid the infamous "warbler neck." Males sing a buzzy *I'm-so-la-zee*, which is the opposite of their energetic behavior. Males and females look so different from each other that they were once believed to be separate species, even by John James Audubon. Unlike some other warblers, which can be confusing to identify in the fall, the male Black-throated Blue retains the same black, blue, and white plumage year-round.

Male is dark blue above and white below with a black face and throat extending down the flanks. Note the white square or "handkerchief" on wings.

Female grayish olive all over with minor hints of blue shining through on the wings and tail. White "handkerchief" on wings diagnostic.

Palm Warbler

Setophaga palmarum

L 5″ | **WS** 8″

A short-distance migrant, many Palm Warblers overwinter in the southeastern U.S. and Gulf Coast states and breed across Canada and the extreme northern U.S. In Ohio they are common passage migrants from mid-April through May in the spring and from September to October in the fall. Palm Warblers feed primarily on the ground or in low vegetation, habitually wagging their tail up and down. There are two subspecies, the "Western" which is common in Ohio, and the "Eastern" which has more extensive yellow on the underparts. The latter migrates mainly along the Atlantic Coast and is a rare visitor to Ohio. Their song resembles a slower Chipping Sparrow trill.

"Western" subspecies common in Ohio. Note rusty cap, yellow throat, supercilium, and undertail coverts.

"Eastern" subspecies rare in Ohio. Like "Western" but extensive yellow on underparts extending from throat to tail.

Pine Warbler

Setophaga pinus

L 5" | **WS** 8"

The Pine Warbler, as its name suggests, is a pine specialist. One of the first warblers to arrive in spring, Pine Warblers migrate through Ohio throughout April and into early May. Within the state, their breeding population is restricted from Cincinnati northeastward to Columbus and Cleveland. The only population west of this line is around the Oak Openings Metro Park near Toledo. Other reliable breeding areas include Shawnee State Park, Mohican State Forest, and Cuyahoga Valley National Park, where they breed in conifer and mixed deciduous/conifer forests. Their song is like Chipping Sparrow but slower and sweeter. Fall migration lasts from September to mid-October. A hardy species, Pine Warblers are regularly found overwintering in the state and often show up at suet feeders in the middle of winter.

Large with a sturdy bill. Adult male has olive-yellow back, head, and breast and a brighter yellow throat. Two obvious white wing bars. Female (not pictured) similar but less extensive yellow.

Immature can be very nondescript lacking any coloration. Note broken eye ring and two white wing bays.

Yellow-rumped Warbler

Setophaga coronata

L 5" | **WS** 9"

Without a doubt, the Yellow-rumped Warbler is the most
abundant migrant warbler in Ohio. In spring large numbers
pass through the state between April and early to mid-May
sometimes outnumbering all other warblers combined. They'll
turn up just about anywhere in parks, gardens, woodlands,
shrubby fields, and even urban environments. Fall migration
typically begins early September and peters down by mid-
November. Yellow-rumped Warblers are also one of the hardiest
species of warbler with a good number choosing to overwinter
in Ohio's harsh winter. At this time of year, they feed on fruits
and berries, including from poison ivy. The occasional bird
will even visit a suet feeder. Their sharp *chek* call is commonly
heard throughout the year while in spring they'll sing a sweet
whistled warble.

Adult male is blue-gray above and
white below with a black mask, white
throat, bold black streaks down the
breast, and yellow patches on the
sides and rump. Adult female like
male but duller overall but still has
diagnostic yellow side patches and
rump. In winter more brownish and
streaky overall retaining diagnostic
yellow side patches and rump.

Yellow-throated Warbler

Setophaga dominica

L 5" | **WS** 8"

Ohio lies at the northern limit of the breeding range for the Yellow-throated Warbler. Historically called the "Sycamore Warbler" for their preference to nest along creeks and rivers lined with tall sycamore trees, they will also utilize stands of native pines in southern Ohio. One of the earliest warblers to return in spring, many are on territory in southern Ohio in April. In recent years they have slowly expanded their range northward. Yellow-throated Warblers are now found throughout Ohio but remain mostly absent from the northernmost tier of the state except in Cuyahoga Valley National Park and a few localized sites near Cleveland and Toledo. Most have departed the state by the end of October.

Attractive larger warbler with a distinctive yellow throat, black face mask, white eyebrow and two white wing bars.

Prairie Warbler

Setophaga discolor

L 4" | **WS** 7"

Another southern breeder, Prairie Warblers expanded their range north during the twentieth century and are now locally common breeders in southern and eastern Ohio. Contrary to their name, they do not breed in prairies, but instead in second-growth habitats supporting a mix of shrubs and young saplings including hillside cutovers. Prairie Warblers arrive in mid-April when their quick series of ascending buzzes can be heard. By mid-July they are silent and infrequently detected, but some linger through September before departing to Florida and the Caribbean for the winter.

Small, mostly yellow warbler. Upperparts are olive-green with a chestnut back patch. Underparts bright yellow with bold black streaks down the flanks. Face striped black and yellow. Female similar but duller.

Black-throated Green Warbler

Setophaga virens

L 5" | **WS** 8"

The appropriately named Black-throated Green Warbler is a common migrant and localized summer breeder in Ohio. Between mid-April and late May large numbers pass through Ohio with good concentrations occurring along Lake Erie. Preferring mature hemlock and mixed hemlock/deciduous forests within the state, Black-throated Green Warblers breed mainly in northeastern Ohio where their habitat is most prevalent. Elsewhere in the state, they breed at Mohican State Forest, Hocking Hills State Park, Clear Creek Metro Park, and Beaver Creek State Park to name a few. Two song types are commonly heard, one is a buzzy *zee, zee, zee, zoo, zee* more often heard during migration and a variation of *zoo, zee, zoo, zoo, zee*. Numbers surge again during fall migration from September through October.

Adult male has a black throat, which extends down the flanks as broad streaks. Back is green and face is yellow with a dusky ear patch.

Female like male but has a white throat and less extensive black markings. Immature is not much different than female, but typically has even less black.

Canada Warbler

Cardellina canadensis

L 5" | **WS** 8"

One of the last warblers to arrive in spring, the northward migration of the Canada Warbler peaks from mid- to late May in Ohio. Males sing a pleasant song starting with a chip and ending in a series of rising and falling notes. To some birders the song resembles a Common Yellowthroat in the wrong habitat. Not as common as most other warblers, and declining, a few remain in the state during the summer to breed. Although they have nested at several sites around northern Ohio in the past, in recent years they have been mostly restricted to the mature hemlock gorges of Mohican State Forest. Fall migration occurs from late August through September when they depart their Canadian and northern U.S. breeding grounds for their South American wintering grounds.

Medium-sized warbler and energetic. Adult male blue-gray above, yellow below, with obvious black necklace and bold yellow eye ring. Female like male but less black on face and fainter necklace.

Wilson's Warbler

Cardellina pusilla

L 4" | **WS** 6"

A little warbler on too much caffeine, the Wilson's Warbler is probably the most energetic and acrobatic warbler of them all. From their wintering grounds in Mexico and Central America, Wilson's Warblers head north to their Canadian breeding grounds passing through Ohio from May to early June, generally later than other species. Fortunately, these tiny warblers tend to feed at lower levels offering a better chance to get a view as they zip around after insects. At first glance the male may look like a Yellow Warbler until you see the little black spot on top of the male's head. Singing males give a sweet rapid series of notes, pause for several seconds, and repeat. Fall migrants return through between August and October.

Male is mostly yellow with a black cap.

Female and immature entirely yellow with an olive crown replacing the black crown in the male.

Summer Tanager

Piranga rubra

L 7" | **WS** 11"

The striking Summer Tanager is the only entirely red bird
in North America. This southern tanager is at its northern
breeding limits in Ohio where they occur mainly in southern
Ohio in addition to Mohican State Forest and Oak Openings Metro Park. Present in the state from late April through
October, they are more localized compared to the far more
common and widespread Scarlet Tanager, which can differentiated by its black wings. Preferring mature deciduous
woodlands and mixed deciduous pine woods, Summer Tanagers
avoid young second-growth habitat. A canopy species, they
spend much of their time high in trees and are best detected by
their robin-like song. These two species can sound similar, so
listening for the Summer's *pit-a-tuck* call will help greatly.

Stocky, big-headed, and
thick bill. Breeding male
entirely vermilion red.

Immature male is splotchy red and yellow. The amount of red depends on how far their molt has progressed.

Female and immature entirely yellow with a pale bill.

Scarlet Tanager

Piranga olivacea

L 7" | **WS** 11"

The brightly beautiful Scarlet Tanager overwinters in South America and begins arriving in mid-April and by May, they are common throughout Ohio's mature deciduous woodlands where they can be found high up in the canopy. A robin with a seemingly sore throat is more likely this species, which has a raspy robin-like song. They also will produce a distinctive *chip-burr* call from above. By the end of October, Scarlet Tanagers will be on their way back to South America.

Male scarlet with black wings and tail and a blunt-tipped bill.

Female and immature soft yellow with darker wings.

Northern Cardinal

Cardinalis cardinalis

L 9" | **WS** 11"

The familiar Northern Cardinal is Ohio's official state bird and is abundant statewide. Cardinals can be found in a variety of habitats, including parks, cemeteries, backyards, woodlands, dense thickets, and brushy margins of wetlands. With their strong conical bills, they are also one of the most regular visitors to birdfeeders where they feed on sunflower seeds. Both male and female cardinals sing a variety of songs, most frequently *birdie, birdie, birdie* or *we-cheer, we, we, we-cheer*. They'll also give a song or calls that sound like they were taken straight out of a "Star Wars" movie. Interestingly, Northern Cardinals were not always common in Ohio and have slowly shifted their range northward over the last few hundred years.

Male all red with a black face and throat and thick seed-eating bill. Note the crest which can lie flat or stand erect.

Female is brown overall with hints of red in the crest, wings, and tail. Immature (not pictured) is all brown and dark-billed.

Rose-breasted Grosbeak
Pheucticus ludovicianus

L 8" | **WS** 12"

The Rose-breasted Grosbeak is a common migrant and summer breeding resident in Ohio from April to October. Occurring in fairly open deciduous forest and forest edge, also in parks and backyards. Females build a rather flimsy nest in a tree or large shrub, often poorly enough to see the eggs through the bottom. Rose-breasted Grosbeaks regularly visit bird feeders where they are especially attracted to sunflower seeds. Their song is often described as a drunken American Robin—quite melodic with sweet whistles but slurred and overly happy. They'll also produce a sharp *chink*.

Male has a black head, back, and wings with white wing patches. Underparts are white with a distinctive red breast.

Female quite different but has typical large triangular bill. Underparts heavily streaked. Note the white eyebrow and pale bill.

Blue Grosbeak

Passerina caerulea

L 6" | **WS** 11"

An uncommon migrant and localized breeder, Blue Grosbeaks are typically a southern species that barely reaches Ohio. In spring, they begin arriving by late April through May. Breeding is mainly restricted from Columbus south in addition to the Oak Openings Metro Park region near Toledo and the Amish communities south of Wooster and Canton. Habitat preference includes dense thickets, brushy corridors, and forest edge scrub. Males will perch conspicuously on top of a tree and sing a rich jumbled warble. A metallic *kink* call is presumably given as an alarm. Most will depart the state by the end of October.

Male a vibrant blue overall with chestnut wing bars, and black around a large triangular pale bill.

Female and immature cinnamon brown with brown wing bars. Note large triangular bill and unmarked underparts.

Indigo Bunting

Passerina cyanea

L 5" | **WS** 8"

A widespread summer breeding resident throughout Ohio, the Indigo Bunting thrives in brushy woodland edges, overgrown fields, and other brushy thickets. These pint-sized deep-blue buntings begin arriving in late April and are especially common during May when local breeders are joined by migrants continuing north. Their song is like the American Goldfinch's, an energetic series of high-pitched notes, but in repeated pairs often described as *what! what! where! where! see it– see it–* The song is commonly heard spring and summer long where they are nesting. Migrants and local residents typically depart the state by the end of October.

Small, sparrow-sized vibrant deep-blue bunting.

Female and nonbreeding male very finch-like. Entirely brownish with faint streaking on the breast and a touch of blue on the wings.

Dickcissel
Spiza americana

L 6" | **WS** 10"

The Dickcissel is an inhabitant of grasslands, prairies, and hayfields in the Great Plains. After the removal of forests in the Great Lakes region in the nineteenth century, Dickcissels expanded eastward into Ohio. They remain uncommon to rare with their numbers fluctuating drastically from year to year. Dickcissels tend to be vocal, perched on fence posts or a short shrub where they sing their namesake, a buzzy *dick-dick-ciss-ciss-ciss*. They are most abundant in the western portion of the state and are nearly absent from south-central Ohio and north along the eastern border. Present from May through August, they are rare outside this time period but have been recorded in Ohio every month of the year

Large and sparrowlike. Adult male has rusty shoulders, a black V on throat, yellow breast, and white underparts. Large conical bill is complimented by a yellowish supercilium and malar stripe.

Female similar to male but lacks the black V on throat.

House Sparrow
Passer domesticus

L 6" | **WS** 9"

Non-native, abundant, and devastating to our local birdlife, the House Sparrow was introduced to Ohio in 1861 when they were released in Cleveland, Cincinnati, and Warren followed by additional releases elsewhere in the state in subsequent years. By 1900, they were abundant throughout the state. As House Sparrows increased, Eastern Bluebirds, Tufted Titmice, and House Wrens were thought to suffer by competition with this aggressive bird for nesting sites. Today, although this sparrow remains abundant in both the rural and urban U.S., the population has declined steadily; it remains a threat to native birds. Commonly heard, the males sing a series of *chirrup* notes repeatedly.

Breeding male has a gray crown, chestnut nape, and white cheeks with a black neck and bib.

In winter, black throat patch on male not as extensive.

Female lacks the black bib. Otherwise brownish overall with a buff, black and brown striped back and a light brown eyebrow.

Acknowledgments

Over the years I have been fortunate to have some of the finest people around me and with their support, knowledge, and friendship, I have now authored my first book. While I have had countless mentors and peers over the years, I want to give special recognition to some of those who have had a lasting impact on me.

There is no better way to start than giving my thanks to my amazing parents, Dallas and Darlene Kistler. Ever since I started birding at age ten, they have supported me in every way imaginable whether being my wheels before I could drive, allowing me to convert family vacations into birding trips, and putting up with a kid who had turned a hobby into an obsession.

Some of those who took me under their wings in the early years include Carole Babyak, Jen Brumfield, Delores Cole, Sheri DeHaven, Linda Gilbert, Tami Gingrich, Andy Jones, Paula Lozano, Jim McCormac, Larry Richardson, Larry Rosche, and Bill Thompson III.

Soon I was heavily involved with young birder camps and programs where I learned a great deal from Jennie Duberstein, Jeff & Liz Gordon, Michael O'Brian and Louise Zemaitis.

My "bird parents" Kim and Kenn Kaufman, I am forever grateful for everything the two of them have done for me and I would be nowhere near where I am today without their support.

And of course I can't forget about my amazing wife Billi Krochuk who helped and supported me throughout the entire process of writing this field guide.

Lastly, George Scott and the rest of the Scott & Nix team for the opportunity to author this field guide and for being patient with a first-time author.

Scott & Nix Acknowledgments

Many thanks to Jeffrey A. and Liz Gordon, Ted Floyd, John Lowry, and everyone at the American Birding Association for their good work. Special thanks to Curt Matthews and Joe Matthews at Independent Book Publishers (IPG) along with their colleagues. Thanks to Alan Poole, Miyoko Chu, and especially Kevin J. McGowan at the Cornell Lab of Ornithology. We give special thanks to Brian E. Small for his extraordinary photographs and to all the others whose images illuminate this guide. We thank Paul Hess for his work on the manuscript; Paul Pianin for helping with layout and proofing the galleys; James Montalbano of Terminal Design for his typefaces; Charles Nix for design; and René Nedelkoff and Porter Print Group for help in shepherding this book through print production.

Image Credits

(T) = Top, (B) = Bottom, (L) = Left, (R) = Right; pages with multiple images from one source are indicated by a single credit.

XIII–XXXIII Brian E. Small. 2–18 Brian E. Small. 19 Alan Murphy (T), Brian E. Small (B). 20–40 Brian E. Small. 41 Alan Murphy (T), Brian E. Small (B). 42–45 Brian E. Small. 46 Brian E. Small (T), Joseph Fuhrman (B). 47–48 Brian E. Small. 49 Alan Murphy (T), Brian E. Small (B). 50–55 Brian E. Small. 56 Jacob Spendelow. 57–78 Brian E. Small. 79 Bob Steele (T), Brian E. Small (B). 80–82 Brian E. Small. 83 Brian E. Small (T), Jacob Spendelow (B). 84–94 Brian E. Small. 95 Brian E. Small (T), Jim Zipp (B). 96 Jacob Spendelow. 97–110 Brian E. Small. 111 Brian E. Small (T), Jacob Spendelow (B). 112–113 Brian E. Small. 114 Jim Zipp. 115 Mike Danzenbaker (T), Jacob Spendelow (B). 116–145 Brian E. Small. 146 Alan Murphy. 147–148 Brian E. Small. 149 Alan Murphy (L), Brian E. Small (R). 150 Brian E. Small. 151 Jim Zipp (T), Jerry Liguori (B). 152 Jim Zipp. 153 Brian E. Small. 154 Alan Murphy. 155–163 Brian E. Small. 164 Brian E. Small (L), Alan Murphy (R). 165–166 Brian E. Small. 167 Jim Zipp. 168 R. Curtis/VIREO (L), Brian E. Small (R). 169–170 Brian E. Small. 171 Brian E. Small (L), Alan Murphy (R). 172–196 Brian E. Small. 197 Alan Murphy (L), Bob Steele (R). 198–226 Brian E. Small. 227 Brian E. Small (T), Jim Zipp (B). 228 Jim Zipp. 229–234 Brian E. Small. 235 Jacob Spendelow. 236–237 Brian E. Small. 238 Brian E. Small (T), Jim Zipp, (B). 239 George L. Armistead (T), Alan Murphy (B). 240–249 Brian E. Small. 250 Brian E. Small (T), Robert Royse (B). 251–270 Brian E. Small. 271 Brian E. Small (T), Jared Mizanin (B). 272 Brian E. Small. 273 Bob Steele (T), Jim Zipp (B). 274 R. Curtis/VIREO, (L), Brian E. Small (R). 275–294 Brian E. Small. 295 Michael L. P. Retter (T), Brian E. Small (B). 296–300 Brian E. Small. 301 Bob Steele (T), Brian E. Small (B). 302 Brian E. Small. 303 Sam Galick (T), Brian E. Small (B). 304 Brian E. Small. 305 Bob Steele (T), Brian E. Small (B). 306–325 Brian E. Small.

Official Ohio Ornithological Society Ohio Bird Checklist

The official Ohio checklist currently (July, 2018) stands at 433 species.

The checklist follows the nomenclature and taxonomic sequence of the Fifty-ninth Supplement to the American Ornithologists' Union *Check-List of North American Birds* (July 2018).

ANATIDAE

- ☐ Black-bellied Whistling-Duck
- ☐ Fulvous Whistling-Duck
- ☐ Snow Goose
- ☐ Ross's Goose
- ☐ Greater White-fronted Goose
- ☐ Brant
- ☐ Cackling Goose
- ☐ Canada Goose
- ☐ Mute Swan
- ☐ Trumpeter Swan
- ☐ Tundra Swan
- ☐ Wood Duck
- ☐ Garganey
- ☐ Blue-winged Teal
- ☐ Cinnamon Teal
- ☐ Northern Shoveler
- ☐ Gadwall
- ☐ Eurasian Wigeon
- ☐ American Wigeon
- ☐ American Black Duck
- ☐ Mallard
- ☐ Northern Pintail
- ☐ Green-winged Teal
- ☐ Canvasback
- ☐ Redhead
- ☐ Ring-necked Duck
- ☐ Tufted Duck
- ☐ Greater Scaup
- ☐ Lesser Scaup
- ☐ King Eider
- ☐ Common Eider
- ☐ Harlequin Duck
- ☐ Surf Scoter
- ☐ White-winged Scoter
- ☐ Black Scoter
- ☐ Long-tailed Duck
- ☐ Bufflehead
- ☐ Common Goldeneye
- ☐ Barrow's Goldeneye
- ☐ Hooded Merganser
- ☐ Common Merganser
- ☐ Red-breasted Merganser
- ☐ Ruddy Duck

ODONTOPHORIDAE

- ☐ Northern Bobwhite

PHASIANIDAE

- ☐ Gray Partridge
- ☐ Ring-necked Pheasant
- ☐ Ruffed Grouse
- ☐ Greater Prairie-Chicken
- ☐ Wild Turkey

PODICIPEDIDAE

- ☐ Pied-billed Grebe
- ☐ Horned Grebe
- ☐ Red-necked Grebe
- ☐ Eared Grebe
- ☐ Western Grebe

COLUMBIDAE

- ☐ Rock Pigeon
- ☐ Eurasian Collared-Dove
- ☐ Passenger Pigeon
- ☐ Common Ground-Dove
- ☐ White-winged Dove
- ☐ Mourning Dove

CUCULIDAE

- ☐ Yellow-billed Cuckoo
- ☐ Black-billed Cuckoo
- ☐ Smooth-billed Ani
- ☐ Groove-billed Ani

CAPRIMULGIDAE

- ☐ Common Nighthawk
- ☐ Chuck-will's-widow
- ☐ Eastern Whip-poor-will

APODIDAE

- ☐ Chimney Swift
- ☐ White-throated Swift

TROCHILIDAE

- ☐ Mexican Violetear
- ☐ Ruby-throated Hummingbird
- ☐ Anna's Hummingbird
- ☐ Rufous Hummingbird
- ☐ Allen's Hummingbird
- ☐ Calliope Hummingbird

RALLIDAE

- ☐ Yellow Rail
- ☐ Black Rail
- ☐ King Rail
- ☐ Virginia Rail
- ☐ Sora
- ☐ Purple Gallinule
- ☐ Common Gallinule
- ☐ American Coot

GRUIDAE

- ☐ Sandhill Crane
- ☐ Whooping Crane

RECURVIROSTRIDAE

- ☐ Black-necked Stilt
- ☐ American Avocet

CHARADRIIDAE

- [ ] Northern Lapwing
- [ ] Black-bellied Plover
- [ ] American Golden-Plover
- [ ] Snowy Plover
- [ ] Wilson's Plover
- [ ] Semipalmated Plover
- [ ] Piping Plover
- [ ] Killdeer

SCOLOPACIDAE

- [ ] Upland Sandpiper
- [ ] Whimbrel
- [ ] Eskimo Curlew
- [ ] Long-billed Curlew
- [ ] Hudsonian Godwit
- [ ] Marbled Godwit
- [ ] Ruddy Turnstone
- [ ] Red Knot
- [ ] Ruff
- [ ] Sharp-tailed Sandpiper
- [ ] Stilt Sandpiper
- [ ] Curlew Sandpiper
- [ ] Red-necked Stint
- [ ] Sanderling
- [ ] Dunlin
- [ ] Purple Sandpiper
- [ ] Baird's Sandpiper
- [ ] Least Sandpiper
- [ ] White-rumped Sandpiper
- [ ] Buff-breasted Sandpiper
- [ ] Pectoral Sandpiper
- [ ] Semipalmated Sandpiper
- [ ] Western Sandpiper
- [ ] Short-billed Dowitcher
- [ ] Long-billed Dowitcher
- [ ] Eurasian Woodcock
- [ ] American Woodcock
- [ ] Wilson's Snipe
- [ ] Spotted Sandpiper
- [ ] Solitary Sandpiper
- [ ] Spotted Redshank
- [ ] Greater Yellowlegs
- [ ] Willet
- [ ] Lesser Yellowlegs
- [ ] Wilson's Phalarope
- [ ] Red-necked Phalarope
- [ ] Red Phalarope

STERCORARIIDAE

- [ ] Pomarine Jaeger
- [ ] Parasitic Jaeger
- [ ] Long-tailed Jaeger

ALCIDAE

- [ ] Thick-billed Murre
- [ ] Black Guillemot
- [ ] Long-billed Murrelet
- [ ] Ancient Murrelet
- [ ] Atlantic Puffin

LARIDAE

- [ ] Black-legged Kittiwake
- [ ] Ivory Gull
- [ ] Sabine's Gull
- [ ] Bonaparte's Gull
- [ ] Black-headed Gull
- [ ] Little Gull
- [ ] Ross's Gull
- [ ] Laughing Gull
- [ ] Franklin's Gull
- [ ] Black-tailed Gull
- [ ] Heermann's Gull
- [ ] Mew Gull
- [ ] Ring-billed Gull
- [ ] California Gull
- [ ] Herring Gull
- [ ] Iceland Gull
- [ ] Lesser Black-backed Gull
- [ ] Glaucous Gull
- [ ] Great Black-backed Gull
- [ ] Kelp Gull
- [ ] Sooty Tern
- [ ] Least Tern
- [ ] Large-billed Tern
- [ ] Caspian Tern
- [ ] Black Tern
- [ ] Common Tern
- [ ] Arctic Tern
- [ ] Forster's Tern
- [ ] Royal Tern

GAVIIDAE

- [ ] Red-throated Loon
- [ ] Arctic Loon
- [ ] Pacific Loon
- [ ] Common Loon

HYDROBATIDAE

- [ ] Leach's Storm-Petrel

PROCELLARIIDAE

- [ ] Black-capped Petrel

CICONIIDAE

- [ ] Wood Stork

FREGATIDAE

- [ ] Magnificent Frigatebird

SULIDAE

- [ ] Northern Gannet

PHALACROCORACIDAE

- [ ] Neotropic Cormorant
- [ ] Great Cormorant
- [ ] Double-crested Cormorant

ANHINGIDAE

- [ ] Anhinga

PELECANIDAE

- [ ] American White Pelican
- [ ] Brown Pelican

ARDEIDAE

- [ ] American Bittern
- [ ] Least Bittern
- [ ] Great Blue Heron
- [ ] Great Egret
- [ ] Snowy Egret
- [ ] Little Blue Heron
- [ ] Tricolored Heron
- [ ] Reddish Egret
- [ ] Cattle Egret
- [ ] Green Heron
- [ ] Black-crowned Night-Heron
- [ ] Yellow-crowned Night-Heron

THRESKIORNITHIDAE

- [ ] White Ibis
- [ ] Glossy Ibis
- [ ] White-faced Ibis
- [ ] Roseate Spoonbill

CATHARTIDAE

- [ ] Black Vulture
- [ ] Turkey Vulture

PANDIONIDAE

- [ ] Osprey

ACCIPITRIDAE

- [ ] Swallow-tailed Kite

- ☐ Golden Eagle
- ☐ Northern Harrier
- ☐ Sharp-shinned Hawk
- ☐ Cooper's Hawk
- ☐ Northern Goshawk
- ☐ Bald Eagle
- ☐ Mississippi Kite
- ☐ Harris's Hawk
- ☐ Red-shouldered Hawk
- ☐ Broad-winged Hawk
- ☐ Swainson's Hawk
- ☐ Red-tailed Hawk
- ☐ Rough-legged Hawk

TYTONIDAE

- ☐ Barn Owl

STRIGIDAE

- ☐ Eastern Screech-Owl
- ☐ Great Horned Owl
- ☐ Snowy Owl
- ☐ Northern Hawk Owl
- ☐ Burrowing Owl
- ☐ Barred Owl
- ☐ Great Gray Owl
- ☐ Long-eared Owl
- ☐ Short-eared Owl
- ☐ Boreal Owl
- ☐ Northern Saw-whet Owl

ALCEDINIDAE

- ☐ Belted Kingfisher

PICIDAE

- ☐ Red-headed Woodpecker
- ☐ Red-bellied Woodpecker
- ☐ Yellow-bellied Sapsucker
- ☐ Red-naped Sapsucker
- ☐ Black-backed Woodpecker
- ☐ Downy Woodpecker
- ☐ Red-cockaded Woodpecker
- ☐ Hairy Woodpecker
- ☐ Northern Flicker
- ☐ Pileated Woodpecker
- ☐ Ivory-billed Woodpecker

FALCONIDAE

- ☐ Crested Caracara
- ☐ American Kestrel
- ☐ Merlin

- ☐ Gyrfalcon
- ☐ Peregrine Falcon
- ☐ Prairie Falcon

PSITTACIDAE

- ☐ Carolina Parakeet

TYRANNIDAE

- ☐ Great Crested Flycatcher
- ☐ Western Kingbird
- ☐ Eastern Kingbird
- ☐ Scissor-tailed Flycatcher
- ☐ Olive-sided Flycatcher
- ☐ Eastern Wood-Pewee
- ☐ Yellow-bellied Flycatcher
- ☐ Acadian Flycatcher
- ☐ Alder Flycatcher
- ☐ Willow Flycatcher
- ☐ Least Flycatcher
- ☐ Gray Flycatcher
- ☐ Dusky Flycatcher
- ☐ Eastern Phoebe
- ☐ Say's Phoebe
- ☐ Vermilion Flycatcher

LANIIDAE

- ☐ Loggerhead Shrike
- ☐ Northern Shrike

VIREONIDAE

- ☐ White-eyed Vireo
- ☐ Bell's Vireo
- ☐ Yellow-throated Vireo
- ☐ Blue-headed Vireo
- ☐ Philadelphia Vireo
- ☐ Warbling Vireo
- ☐ Red-eyed Vireo

CORVIDAE

- ☐ Blue Jay
- ☐ Black-billed Magpie
- ☐ American Crow
- ☐ Fish Crow
- ☐ Common Raven

ALAUDIDAE

- ☐ Horned Lark

HIRUNDINIDAE

- ☐ Purple Martin
- ☐ Tree Swallow
- ☐ Violet-green Swallow

- ☐ Northern Rough-winged Swallow
- ☐ Bank Swallow
- ☐ Cliff Swallow
- ☐ Cave Swallow
- ☐ Barn Swallow

PARIDAE

- ☐ Carolina Chickadee
- ☐ Black-capped Chickadee
- ☐ Boreal Chickadee
- ☐ Tufted Titmouse

SITTIDAE

- ☐ Red-breasted Nuthatch
- ☐ White-breasted Nuthatch
- ☐ Brown-headed Nuthatch

CERTHIIDAE

- ☐ Brown Creeper

TROGLODYTIDAE

- ☐ Rock Wren
- ☐ House Wren
- ☐ Winter Wren
- ☐ Sedge Wren
- ☐ Marsh Wren
- ☐ Carolina Wren
- ☐ Bewick's Wren

POLIOPTILIDAE

- ☐ Blue-gray Gnatcatcher

REGULIDAE

- ☐ Golden-crowned Kinglet
- ☐ Ruby-crowned Kinglet

MUSCICAPIDAE

- ☐ Northern Wheatear

TURDIDAE

- ☐ Eastern Bluebird
- ☐ Mountain Bluebird
- ☐ Townsend's Solitaire
- ☐ Veery
- ☐ Gray-cheeked Thrush
- ☐ Swainson's Thrush
- ☐ Hermit Thrush
- ☐ Wood Thrush
- ☐ American Robin
- ☐ Varied Thrush

MIMIDAE

- [ ] Gray Catbird
- [ ] Brown Thrasher
- [ ] Northern Mockingbird

STURNIDAE

- [ ] European Starling

BOMBYCILLIDAE

- [ ] Bohemian Waxwing
- [ ] Cedar Waxwing

PASSERIDAE

- [ ] House Sparrow
- [ ] Eurasian Tree Sparrow

MOTACILLIDAE

- [ ] American Pipit
- [ ] Sprague's Pipit

FRINGILLIDAE

- [ ] Brambling
- [ ] Evening Grosbeak
- [ ] Pine Grosbeak
- [ ] Gray-crowned Rosy-Finch
- [ ] House Finch
- [ ] Purple Finch
- [ ] Common Redpoll
- [ ] Hoary Redpoll
- [ ] Red Crossbill
- [ ] White-winged Crossbill
- [ ] Pine Siskin
- [ ] American Goldfinch

CALCARIIDAE

- [ ] Lapland Longspur
- [ ] Smith's Longspur
- [ ] Snow Bunting

PASSERELLIDAE

- [ ] Green-tailed Towhee
- [ ] Spotted Towhee
- [ ] Eastern Towhee
- [ ] Cassin's Sparrow
- [ ] Bachman's Sparrow
- [ ] American Tree Sparrow
- [ ] Chipping Sparrow
- [ ] Clay-colored Sparrow
- [ ] Field Sparrow
- [ ] Vesper Sparrow
- [ ] Lark Sparrow
- [ ] Black-throated Sparrow

- [ ] Lark Bunting
- [ ] Savannah Sparrow
- [ ] Grasshopper Sparrow
- [ ] Baird's Sparrow
- [ ] Henslow's Sparrow
- [ ] LeConte's Sparrow
- [ ] Nelson's Sparrow
- [ ] Fox Sparrow
- [ ] Song Sparrow
- [ ] Lincoln's Sparrow
- [ ] Swamp Sparrow
- [ ] White-throated Sparrow
- [ ] Harris's Sparrow
- [ ] White-crowned Sparrow
- [ ] Golden-crowned Sparrow
- [ ] Dark-eyed Junco

ICTERIIDAE

- [ ] Yellow-breasted Chat

ICTERIDAE

- [ ] Yellow-headed Blackbird
- [ ] Bobolink
- [ ] Eastern Meadowlark
- [ ] Western Meadowlark
- [ ] Orchard Oriole
- [ ] Bullock's Oriole
- [ ] Baltimore Oriole
- [ ] Red-winged Blackbird
- [ ] Brown-headed Cowbird
- [ ] Rusty Blackbird
- [ ] Brewer's Blackbird
- [ ] Common Grackle
- [ ] Great-tailed Grackle

PARULIDAE

- [ ] Ovenbird
- [ ] Worm-eating Warbler
- [ ] Louisiana Waterthrush
- [ ] Northern Waterthrush
- [ ] Golden-winged Warbler
- [ ] Blue-winged Warbler
- [ ] Black-and-white Warbler
- [ ] Prothonotary Warbler
- [ ] Swainson's Warbler
- [ ] Tennessee Warbler
- [ ] Orange-crowned Warbler
- [ ] Nashville Warbler
- [ ] Connecticut Warbler
- [ ] Mourning Warbler
- [ ] Kentucky Warbler

- [ ] Common Yellowthroat
- [ ] Hooded Warbler
- [ ] American Redstart
- [ ] Kirtland's Warbler
- [ ] Cape May Warbler
- [ ] Cerulean Warbler
- [ ] Northern Parula
- [ ] Magnolia Warbler
- [ ] Bay-breasted Warbler
- [ ] Blackburnian Warbler
- [ ] Yellow Warbler
- [ ] Chestnut-sided Warbler
- [ ] Blackpoll Warbler
- [ ] Black-throated Blue Warbler
- [ ] Palm Warbler
- [ ] Pine Warbler
- [ ] Yellow-rumped Warbler
- [ ] Yellow-throated Warbler
- [ ] Prairie Warbler
- [ ] Black-throated Gray Warbler
- [ ] Townsend's Warbler
- [ ] Black-throated Green Warbler
- [ ] Canada Warbler
- [ ] Wilson's Warbler
- [ ] Painted Redstart

CARDINALIDAE

- [ ] Summer Tanager
- [ ] Scarlet Tanager
- [ ] Western Tanager
- [ ] Northern Cardinal
- [ ] Rose-breasted Grosbeak
- [ ] Black-headed Grosbeak
- [ ] Blue Grosbeak
- [ ] Indigo Bunting
- [ ] Painted Bunting
- [ ] Dickcissel

Species Index

A

Ethan Kistler, a life-long Ohian, began birding at the age of ten. He has traveled to work in bird-related jobs from Ohio to Alaska and led bird tours throughout North America, Europe, and Africa (where he lived for seven years). Previously the director-at-large for the Ohio Ornithological Society, Ethan's main focus now is professional bird guiding. He lives in Trumbull County, Ohio.

Brian E. Small is a full-time professional bird and nature photographer. For more than twenty-five years, he has traveled widely across North America to capture images of birds in their native habitats. He served as the photo editor at *Birding* magazine for fifteen years. Small grew up in Los Angeles, graduated from U.C.L.A. in 1982 and still lives there today with his wife Ana, daughter Nicole, and son Tyler.

Quick Index

See the Species Index for a complete listing of all the birds in the *American Birding Association Field Guide to Birds of Ohio*.